Women Seeking in Men: How to Flirt with Men, Boost your Sexual Intelligence, Learn How to Get the Guy and Seduce Him from the First Date

Steve Perry

© **Copyright**

All rights reserved

This book is targeted towards offering essential details about the subject covered. The publication is being provided with the thought that the publisher is not mandated to render an accounting or other qualified services. If recommendations are needed, professional or legal, a practiced person in the profession ought to be engaged.

In no way is it legal to recreate, duplicate, or transfer any part of this document in either electronic means or printed format. Copying of this publication is strictly prohibited, or storage of this document is not allowed. Unless, with written authorization from the publisher. All rights reserved.

The details supplied herein is specified, to be honest, and constant. Because any liability, in regards to inattention or otherwise, by any usage or abuse of any directions, processes, or policies confined within is the sole and utter obligation of the recipient reader. Under no circumstances will any form of legal duty or blame be held against the publisher for any reparation, damages, or financial loss due to the information herein, either directly or indirectly. The author owns all copyrights not held by the publisher.

The information herein is provided for educational purpose exclusively and is universal. The presentation of the data is without contractual agreement or any kind of warranty assurance.

All trademarks inside this book are for clarifying purposes only and are possessed by the owners themselves, not allied with this document.

Disclaimer

All erudition supplied in this book are specified for educational and academic purpose only. The author is not in any way in charge of any outcomes that emerge from utilizing this book. Constructive efforts have been made to render information that is both precise and effective; however, the author is not to be held answerable for the accuracy or use/misuse of this information.

Foreword

I will like to thank you for taking the very first step of trusting me and deciding to purchase/read this life-transforming book. Thanks for investing your time and resources on this product.

I can assure you of precise outcomes if you will diligently follow the specific blueprint I lay bare in the information handbook you are currently checking out. It has transformed lives, and I strongly believe it will equally transform your own life too.

All the information I provided in this Do It Yourself piece is easy to absorb and practice.

INTRODUCTION

The pages you're about to read expose everything that you need to know to date and have relationships with men successfully.

This book will teach you how men think, date, and mate, so that navigating the dating world will be as easy as changing a lightbulb: just throw out the old one, get a new one, and screw him.

The knowledge in this book can change your life in two significant ways:

1. About ninety percent of the so-called relationship experts are only putting Band-Aids on relationship injuries. They're not teaching women how to check out men well enough to get in hot and healthy relationships. If you listen well enough, a man will most likely tell you everything you ought to know about how he feels about you, what he's doing, what he's doing next, I will teach you how to check out these signs.

2. Women who genuinely know men can beat them at their own game, and take the faster way to discover pleasing relationships. All women can cover their minds alongside bad-boy behavior and use it to their benefit in any connection.

This book is written to teach you how to achieve this too. It's a matter of emotional empowerment, enabling you to take action, which will transform the way you live and love.

Courting is like a dance: men lead, and women follow. Proactive women, on the other hand, step on some toes when necessary and make that dance last for years. This book will help women be dynamic by giving them the truth and the knowledge of the power to lead a relationship in whatever direction that suits them.

The primary objective of this book is not like that of any relationship guidance book out there: To get you to know that dating has to do with bringing your self with a new and confident understanding of the way dating works. To get you to know that dating is not about picking someone up or manipulating him. It s something to study, take in, and store at the back of your mind. It s something that ought to become a part of you, something you'll draw on later when you take every opportunity to take charge and meet men face to face as often as possible.

You'll be amazed at the changes you see in your dating life if you make an effort to read this book and apply it to every Mr. Right who comes your way.

CHAPTER ONE

Bad Boy and Nice Guy

Who Is a Bad Boy?

Admit it; you wish to date Bad Boys. Notwithstanding what your mother might have told you, they make the best boyfriends. They're the best, they love women, and they know how to turn you on. Let me describe it.

BadBoy (n.) A captivating, funny, overtly positive man who is hot, in great shape, and high in bed. He is unapologetically "man," loves women, keeps many female friends, and doesn't kiss and tell. He's noncommittal by choice, not by fear. Most important, he prospers on being naughty.

I'd be sugarcoating the definition if I didn't discuss the "bad" part. Such a man is bad because he's "got your number," knows how to manipulate you, and may not view female casualties as an issue. He doesn't often see you as a person, but instead as a problem or a case study. For lots of Bad Boys, the chase is more significant than the catch. The result? Hearts are broken, your need for getting close is ignored, and he's off to his next "mark," remembering you just as an experience.

Examples: Great Hollywood Bad Boys have included George Clooney, Colin Farrell, Johnny Knoxville, Jude Law, Jack

Nicholson, Snoop Dogg, Vince Vaughn, Warren Beatty, and John Mayer.

Bad Boys come in all sizes and shapes. You know when a Bad Boy goes into a place: His confidence and past success with women are exposed in his constant eye contact, his slow, specific rate, and the glaring looks he gets from other men. The women in the space perk up like deer at a water hole. He is instantly king of whatever domain he enters, and he doesn't feel the need to prove himself. He simply is.

Devotion to the Cause.

Bad Boy studies women with the same enthusiasm and devotion that Nobel laureates pursue academia. Instead, he most likely gets something much better, something every man on earth desires: an indisputable capability to seduce women based solely on who he is active. Women are brought in not to his status, bank account, or intelligence; instead, he can charm women strictly based on himself.

The majority of real Bad Boys arc born or reared on occasion, a lucky couple of stumble and inadvertently fall into acting severely as a way to succeed with the opposite sex, summoned to a life invested pursuing the understanding of women.

Why You Must Like Them

There has been all kind of studies done on why women are attracted to this "naughty" part in men. To us, Bad Boys, this is all about clinical chatter. Women mostly have the best chance at doing better if they choose only the strongest alpha males, and men have the best opportunity of spreading if they can draw in many women.

Polygamy went out with the bodice; for this reason, the problem in the dating. You like me, desire my romantic attention, and want me to date you monogamously.

Even if you think you do not like complete Bad Boys, every woman needs a man with an edge to keep her warmed up.

Who He's Not.

I hear the word player considered a lot to describe men who seek out multitudes of women. This is what I'm here to break down for you, and tell you that Bad Boys and players are not the same things- Let me explain:

Player.

-Boasts about his conquests.

-Cares deeply about his." numbers."

-Has cheap air.

-Makes a game out of getting women's phone numbers.

-Has a considerable understanding of women and cares to know only enough to get them into bed.

Bad Boy.

-He is very deceptive and will hardly speak about his private life.

-Delights in exploring different "types" of women.

-Is positive.

-They love women.

Most of the man's ex-girlfriends are still his friends and not longing for his unforeseen death.

In summary, a player often sees women as notches on his bed- He doesn't truly love them, or care to know them. A player wants to get women drunk and benefit from them; he does not bother how a woman is seduced, as long as she goes to bed with him. He sees women as something of a game. The majority of players are wealthier men who prey on gold diggers, intoxicated girls, or unsuspecting women. A player can quickly be the unemployed loser down the block Lord understands he has the time. If you would like to know what to search for to avoid this person, focus here.

How to Spot a Player

- He has more male than female friends.

- He may have money and elegant "props": clothing, automobiles, and watches.

- He's a name-dropper.

- He makes promises he will never keep.

- He starts touching you-- your back, your arm, anywhere-- from the minute you meet, in manner ins which might strike you as far more intimate than your relationship warrants.

- You'll observe something about him is sleazy, even if you can't put your finger on it. Need you to put your finger on it, please wash with hot, soapy water.

Players can eventually be heroes, but it's better to know what you're doing from the get-go. Chances are, you aren't going to be the one to change him, so carry on quickly if you wish to prevent the heartache associated with it.

The Myth of the Nice Guy

Odds are you are likely never to fall for a plain old nice guy. That's not to say that you will not meet an edgy person who is suitable for you. Or that you will not be drawn into an exceptionally polite guy.

In that world called truth, every man has a little Bad Boy in him, and women wouldn't have it any other way.

There's Nothing Nice About Nice.

A nice guy is a kid you wish to pat on the head like a puppy, saying, "Aww, aren't you sweet." He's most likely the friend whom you adore but would never date. The nice guy can't get you hot. Nice people can't even "get" you anywhere. Nice guys, as far as women are concerned, might as well have WELCOME stamped on their heads because you use them as doormats, which is sad because a lot of cute guys would make great partners, other than for one thing: They do not make you feel safe. Or they are excited.

The same reason nature advises you to go for an alpha male is why you can't be drawn into "nice." In life, beautiful equals weak, and weak equals danger. Women wish to feel that they are safe and protected. Even if you're a powerful woman, you still want to be with somebody who's got some halls. No?

Here's how to get a guy with just the right amount of Bad Boyishness.

1. Date different kinds of men from numerous walks of life: business types, imaginative, athletic, outdoorsy, and so on (but do not sleep with any of them).

2. Accurately date outside of what you would consider your regular "type," and start to develop an idea of what you like and don't like; keep a chart, if it helps. Ask yourself what qualities

are most crucial to you. Is he edgy, responsible, polite, a good kisser?

3. If a person makes you hot, then keep dating him, but do not get too emotionally involved right away. Stand back and ask yourself, "What is making me want him so badly?".

4. Compare the men who make you hot with the man you consider a nice guy. You can feel free to use the nice men in your life to keep you busy so that you're not too available for the "hottie" you like. Nice men will not learn to be naughty by your being kind to them; you're doing them a favor!

5. Possibilities are that if he turns you on, he's a "genuine person." Let him know (without saying it!) that you know his desire to be manly. This "acceptance," if you will, will separate you from 90 percent of the female population. Significance, if he's a little rowdy often if he's got a pastime-- a bike, for example-- or even a sport he just has to spend time on," then welcome it, but let him know you will not play second fiddle all the time. In this manner, you're not there as filler between his "man-time" and work. You become part of his man-time.

The fact that you're reading this book means that you are actively looking for details that will better enable you to understand men, and therefore have more fun with the kind of man who gets you hot but not so hot that he burns you. You're on your way! If you pay attention to the advice in this book, I promise you'll be able to manage the hotness.

How Bad Boys Help Bring Out the Best in Women

Bad Boys do not sound right, do they? But you mostly want to be around someone who brings out the best in you, and that often means a guy is misbehaving. These types of men can get your blood boiling and successfully bring out the vibe and spirit in your body. Like each woman has a spicy side of herself, every man has a little devil in him, and women like to use that.

This sometimes causes men to shriek at women in frustration. But allowing these emotions to get out is a good thing. Men rarely do this, and it's just one of the ways women can be more entertaining than men: You should be funny, sensitive, intelligent, talk about your "emotions" and have a dirty sense of humor.

Ways Bad Boys Stir You Up

Allowing a man to tap into your funny side, which your former guy might have been either too stupid or too lazy to try, can be great for both of you. Are you not sure if you are with a Bad Boy or not? A Bad Boy uses some tricks with female friends or girlfriends. Below are some strategies—see if any of them looks familiar:

1. Telling you, "you are beautiful: Every woman is somehow unique in and of herself, and a man can pay special attention to noticing every curve and every mannerism. For example, Some men rarely go for the apparent compliment. Instead, they praise a dimple, the color of her hair, her nose, or the cute way she walks.

Some men compliment a woman about how beautiful she is just in a way that is special to her.

2. Encouraging Naughtiness

A guy may encourage the woman he is with to open up about fantasies. He doesn't judge her on what she has done in the past.

He has fun with some mild forms of dirty-talking and playing games. He doesn't kiss and tell.

It's essential for a woman to feel safe feeling naughty, and it's the guy's job to create that safe environment. Women are mostly just as bad as men, but society somehow labels you when you choose to express those types of thoughts, but you should feel safe and open in the bedroom.

3.Occasional Fight

Have you ever met with a man who seems to pick a fight with you for no evident reason? Early in a relationship, a man may often purposefully press a lady's buttons to see what she's made of. You learn a whole lot about a man from how he acts when he's mad.

This is not a way of promoting physical violence, hostility, or unnecessary battling. Some women don't express the way they feel They bottle it up until it is pouring out in a tirade. Just bear in mind: you can't reclaim words, and you 'd better be able to make it if you dish it out.

Everything boils down to the fact that charm, naughtiness, and even fights make both men and women feel active as well as actual. As well as motivating these actions is one of the significant talents of Bad Boys.

CHAPTER TWO

Inside the Man's Mind

It's essential to learn how to take advantage of exactly how men think. This is an excellent way to keep a man.

Looking excellent and dressing with the belief that you desire to bring in men provides a lady alternative. I'll clarify: You've listened to a lot of "beer goggles," when a guy sees a woman as hotter than she truly is since he's intoxicated. If you take benefit of what I've created in this book, men will begin to see you with clarity.

Men don't desire to spend their entire lives with airheads. No matter how sensitive and wise men might be, they are at first brought in by your appearances and sexiness. Look wonderful, and when you've got men circling like sharks on the high seas, it's time to chat some feeling right into them, and get their minds interested in the "rest" of the splendidly intelligent you, from the neck up.

The women who understand and use the most significant facets of their bodies are the ones that have the best choices in guys! Every component of a female's body ought to be made use of to adjust a man. Does that sound severe? My goal is not to externalize you; it's just to inspire you to wind up being an item of need. Peacocks have plumes to attract the contrary sex with, comparable to you, have your appearance. You always need to keep in mind the message you are sending. When you are attempting to draw in and maintain possible companions, you must think about these things.

Home window Dressing

Why would a single lady gown with her good friends or associates in mind? Is she fretted about what various other females will think regarding her?

Whatever the factor, this one technique alone might be killing your lovemaking.

The number one means to increase your possibilities of bring in Mr. Right substantially is to believe hot first > after that style. The looks that are cool and also elegant are, usually, absolutely thrown away on 99.9 percent of the male population. We couldn't care less concerning your Manolo blah Blahniks or Jimmy Choo choo. Stick with Payless; we couldn't care much less.

Take a thing from us: When it involves clothing, guys are enticing as well as comfortable to females, usually because order. We also presume that you such as to recognize what our bodies appear like, so we try using garments that reveal our bodies' shape-- or conceals it, whatever is extra charming.

Some males might not confess it; however, we like the tip of "trampy" in whatever that women wear.) It's pleasant, and it's a turn-on.

Men like a little bit cost-effective: Women that use a little bit of sexual magnetism on their sleeve are ruled out sluts by men; they're considered datable and also smart!

I recognize precisely how persistent women can be in evaluating one another. Keep in mind, they're jealous, and they don't care if you're home alone on a Friday evening. Screw them and also outfit to get rid of males. Guy transforms to look at a hint of sexiness a million times faster than a tip of style. As quickly as you have their attention, you've obtained alternatives, but you need to catch our interest. Overtly stylish females barely grab our interest. We take a look at those girls as high maintenance, and on the unusual celebration that we date one, we're just there to see exactly how they beware of all that stuff.

Those warm garments are not to be kept in your storage room. A guideline: If you do not feel the tingle of raciness when you look in the mirror, then possibilities are you're missing it. In general, it's better to lean in the direction of rowdy if you are trying to meet males.

The Rest of the Closet

If you're genuinely significant about satisfying a guy, then whatever you carry out in the name of style, be it with your hair, your footwear, your underwear, or your garments, need to take the male point of view into account.

I say "account" since nobody desires to cater simply to guys; neither ought to them: if we had our means, females would certainly dress like cheerleaders or place on limited denims as well as sheer storage tank tops all year long. Instead, you want to support your sense of layout with your understanding of what men see.

A Woman's Closet, Designed by Men

Underwears

Some women have often stated that when they wear great underwear, even though nobody might see it, they will undoubtedly stroll and also talk in different ways, sensation in one's bones they have an attractive little trick. If undergarments can do that to a lady-- as well as we currently know just how it impacts men-- then do not you think you should go out as well as get on your own some? You have a whole lot of options, and also, when it comes to lingerie, men like anything.

Shoes

Once more, we do not care. We understand you like them. We do not comprehend why you desire them. All we recognize is that several of you have closets packed with them, and we've figured out that provided that you spend much money and time on them, we can match them to flatter you.

She's so pleasant that she believed he indicated it. Have you ever listened to a man claim, "Well, things that caught my eye was Shirley's footwear? I love those pumps, as well as when I saw them, and I recognized she was the Woman for me"?

There is a particular style of shoes that men see, and also that's high heels. Cheesy, and even not exceptionally sensible in the sands of Miami andL.A., yet males notice without a doubt.

Hair.

Hair, on the other hand, is, sigh, among the sexiest features of a woman. Hair gets us and doesn't let us go. Think of octopus arms. Your texture, color, and style are no matter. Your hair just needs to be clean, tousled, just-out-of-bed appearance. My viewpoint is that most women look sexier with longer hair than much shorter. Men like long, hot hair mostly because we don't have it. Plus, incredibly few women can get away with that brief boy resemblance. Next time you're out in public, check how men look at women with long hair against short.

With the Internet and billions of fashion magazines at your fingertips, you've got plenty of references. Please think sexy and invest the time and cash to get the right do. When in doubt, turn to whichever celeb women are getting the most attention for being sexy, and copy them.

A few more essential tips:

Don't color your hair based on the swatches you got at the paint shop. Other designs to avoid include bad bangs or mullets. Stop cutting your hair short as you age-- there's no need to.

Dresses

Every Woman uses a dress differently. The only mandatory rule is to choose a dress that highlights your best body parts. Whether r you have a beautiful back, amazing thighs, or delicate collarbones, stock up on styles that don't only fit but also showcase those impressive attributes.

Your shape and also elevation identify much of what you'll look great in, yet right here are some basic general rules:

Shorter Girls

- Wear heels. Heels create the impression of longer legs. And also as I've stated, they're hot!

- Buy a dress that slightly sticks, while still allowing your base to relocate rapidly. Examine out the red carpet "best dressed" listings.

Suppose you have some pounds to lose, - Loose cotton dress arc best. They offer males a suggestion of your bottom and legs without a sharp photo. We have vibrant creative imaginations, as well as the guy believes you good-looking, not even worse.

Taller Girls

- Stand up directly, shoulders back, breast-high.

- Wear longer gowns that hug your legs a little bit. You desire an equipped design.

- Pick either heels or apartments, depending on exactly how high you intend to show up.

- Make sure that the dress covers at the very least 60 percent of your skin. You have a large amount of skin, and a little goes a lengthy means.

- As with much shorter girls, loose-fitting, large cotton gowns that cling a little are terrific for women having extra weight.

Bottoms and Tops

Call it your "finest of good luck withstanding me" area. Feel complimentary to match and also blend from the much more "domestic" side of your storage room, yet always keep in mind: It's a jungle out there, and even occasionally, it pays to become a little wild if you wish to sustain!

Glasses

Just make sure you select a fantastic style that flatters your face and keeps the lenses free of eyelashes and also fingerprints. I enjoy chicks in glasses.

CHAPTER THREE

The Secret of Successful Dating for Women

Knowing that not all dates will lead to marital relationships. Often, people make much better friends, but you can never have too many friends, right? Mobile dating for women is much about meeting new people as it is finding true love.

-Do not be too picky. If you do have a list of qualities that each prospective date need to have, you are eliminating entire segments of the population rather than opening yourself as much as possible.

-Be open to new experiences. Not all auspicious dates have to be in a five-star restaurant. Want to attempt new skills, and have a little fun.

Sign up with clubs, go to parties, watch local sports, and look for possible dates somewhere other than the local bar or club. You're far more likely to discover somebody who shares your interests and values if you're participating in them, than if you're propping up a bar counter somewhere!

-Don't hesitate to blind dates. Dating for women is all about meeting as many people as you can, and who better to help you do that than your friends and family - people who know you best? Yes, some might be dreadful, but some will not.

-Make an effort. Even if you're smart, amusing, and downright incredible, if you look like a bag lady, men, who are visual animals, are most likely to run yelling in the opposite directions! Make sure you're well dressed, that your hair is done, and that you always look your best.

As you can see, dating for women is more about you than about your prospective dates. You need to takeout some time to analyze your motives and how you look at dating if you want your dating to be a success. Once you've done that, go out there and meet men - you never know when your soul mate will turn up, but if you're not looking, you might simply miss him!

Keep in mind, while dating for women is everything about unwinding overly high needs from time to time; nevertheless, you ought to know the distinction between being open to possibilities and settling. Settling for less than you are worthy of ought not to be an alternative!

Dating Websites are the most popular and easy way to come in contact with new and fascinating men. With many dating sites on the internet, it can be both complicated and discouraging to know which to use. If you are a lady or woman and you are looking to meet a man who is well established financially, then you need to sign up for dating websites that cater to men who meet specific income guidelines.

Some of the much better ones will allow you to sign up as a user without a membership charge, although you will have restricted access to some extent. This will let you look at the many available single and effective men who have their profiles noted on the website. You can see their photos, their profile details, which will tell you more about who they are and the stuff they are looking for in a girlfriend. The website will enable you to send out a "wink" to let the man know that you are interested in knowing much more about him. This feature will also give them a link to your profile so they can get to know you. Sometimes this causes you to get emails from interested members. Then, if you would like to sign up as a paying member, you can do so to enable you to have many more options. These will consist of the ability to email other members and take part in live chat. Also, many other more sophisticated alternatives will be possible such as search criteria, which can be more particular to what you are seeking in a mate.

Be Authentic: Yes, it is essential to be authentic and real to who you are. When you create your profile, do not misrepresent yourself or say things that aren't true. Yes, you need to create the sleekest and favorable image of yourself as you can. But stay within the specifications of explaining who you are. Explain your interests and your personality. What are you enthusiastic about? What are you seeking in a mate? Don't concentrate on any unfavorable qualities in your profile. Keep everything optimistic and favorable.

-Present Photos: A common mistake lots of women make is publishing photos of themselves that are not current. This is not a wise idea. If you do get to meet, it might turn out to be a disappointing experience because the man might feel that you were not truthful with him. Always use current pictures of yourself that were taken within the last year. The quality of the photos is paramount, as this is the visual element that is critical in gaining potential suitor's attention. The best images are of you alone in a picture, smiling and looking happy. Always list a couple of photos, not a "gallery," possibly four to five images is okay. Do not use photographs showing you and your friend, your children, your pets, and so on. Keep the photos tidy and necessary, a few face pictures, and possibly one or two full-body photos dressed your best.

-Choosing who to call: When you go through the hundreds of options available to you to contact, you have to learn to narrow your focus on what is essential to you in a relationship. The best dating sites enable you to evaluate through many of these needs so that you can find the men you might have many things in common.

Numerous women make the mistake of creating an email that they use over and over to reach out to every man they want to contact. A man will know that such an email is not unique. Your email needs to involve some specific things about the man you are interacting with.

These are just a couple of essential tips on how to have a more compelling online dating experience. Why not begin today and get yourself listed on one of the more reliable dating websites. You would have a good time and enjoy the experience. And who knows, you may just meet the man of your dreams.

How to Understand Men's Communication

"Am I leaping the gun, thinking he's not interested? It just looks as if he truly liked me, and I thought he did why has he not called." Well, I've seen a guy who's not interested, and it looks different from this.

A guy who's not interested is in the room, speaking with somebody else, totally uninformed of your presence. He is not welcoming you over, cooking dinner for you and cuddling you. The most accurate gauge of people's thoughts is their behaviors, so love what he does.

Which brings us to the second point:

"I've never understood why guys do this. I know that I deserve someone to treat me well, and he did that, but I don't know the not calling thing. I guess I just have to move on and keep working on myself and grow with the hope of attracting someone who does call and make plans to spend time with me. Any advice would be appreciated."

Well, here's my question for women reading this: What do you want? Sure, he hasn't called you (yet). And the only thing that indicates is that he hasn't called you (however). But did you have a good time? Do you want to see him again? You have a voice, so use it!

He took the risk of asking you out and already put in the effort to entertain you and take care of you. If you were now on a date with him, would you simply sit there, waiting for him to offer and give once again, while you just take? While he takes all the risk? I've found that many women misconstrue this 'taking of turns' as an absence of interest. Here's a simple way of understanding what's going on: put yourself in the shoes of the person. He's put his ego on the line before now and asked you out.

Otherwise, he's getting no details on your interest level. Better than to wait for you to make the next move.

Picture how you would feel if a man did not call you to say thanks the day after you went dinner for him.

There's a spiritual concept at work here that says that you get more of whatever you concentrate on and give your energy. If you want men to make more home-cooked meals for you, thank them profusely for that. If you want them to call you early and often, call them early and often—energy streams where attention goes.

As Gandhi once stayed, "Be the change you wish to see in the world.

NLP and Dating - For Women Only

Are you a dating coach for women? Let me show you some powerful NLP ideas about techniques to make the journey more straightforward for your clients. A "method" is the way we approach anything in life, from waking up to brushing our teeth to setting about our days and also to dating.

Awareness of what we are doing is the first action. We can then see how others are successful in that direction, discover what they do, and model that technique.

Have you attempted online dating? It is a guessing game and a grab-bag. You see a guy's picture and his description, and by now, you know that there is typically not a reality in marketing.

Say after a couple of dates with these online people; you find somebody fascinating. A number of us women assume that in this age of high-speed internet that high-speed relationships are where it's at. Relations have not changed. There are still the same standard techniques that have been around since those caveman days.

Notably, this means that men love the hunt. If there is not a hunt involved, they feel let down.

As we humans are "wired" in a specific way with feelings and other inner systems of behavior, successful dating for women includes working within this hard-wired system and not thinking of there is something different about this specific guy you are considering.

There is likewise something to think about women's hard-wired methods. When a woman has sexual relations with a man, something takes place biologically that produces a bond with that man. Now, you can go considering that it is not valid that you are different, and perhaps you are among the people who are. If you discover that you have been in a series of failing relationships, and your way is to get physically involved quickly, then possibly it is a great time to assess your strategy.

If you get involved with somebody who you know is not "good enough" for you, and he discards you, you can find yourself in an unusual position of having believed you were too good for him, then he rejects you, so, therefore, you are less than what you thought of him in the first place. If you have dated much, you know what I'm talking about.

Then is the old made "play tough to get" method the best way? It might be something to try out. Experience a new way of dating; see what results you get. Do this like a study, be curious, be outrageous.

You say playing hard to get is not real? Well, if you are enjoying your own life, it is entirely authentic. You will create a powerful allure if you make your life

1. Following your interests that rock your world and finding your life enjoyment will make it, so you are not so readily available for a new man. Let him show you that he is prepared to work for your gracious existence. As the sexual tension constructs, take this time to discover who he is, who his friends are, what his family looks like.

We are not islands. We get involved with the other person, their habits, their people, and that world enter into us.

What are your dating techniques? Are they working for you? If not, think about modeling excellent behavior that will get you your desired result.

Invest carefully on yourself. Be curious. As a question, how can I develop the highest value for my life?

Right & Wrong Attention and the Attraction Gradient

There's a spiritual principle at work here that states that you get more of whatever you focus on and give your energy to. So if you want men to make more home-cooked meals for you, thank them profusely for that. Call them early and frequently if you want them to call you early and often. Energy flows where attention goes.

Now the principle of 'energy flows where attention goes' has been specified in many ways throughout the ages. Among them is the Golden Rule: "Do unto others as you would have them do unto you."

If you desire to be called, call when social commitment needs you-- to say thanks, or to return a call. This is not the same as saying 'inundate the object of your affection with attention from the first second,' which the figure of speech 'call early and often' could be interpreted.

There is a middle course between coquetry ("I'm going to play hard to get, and I'm going to play it well") and stalking somebody with nineteen emails and calls a day, which is the path of the Tao.

What is right for you? TRUST YOUR INSTINCTS.

Why? I can think of two reasons today.

Because you are Woman, the animal with the most finely developed intuition in the entire universe, it's real. Evolution has equipped you with extremely delicate tools for spotting feelings, states of mind, and the totality of a situation, to sum the entire thing up and give you an answer which is frequently very precise.

How accurate? Well, it's kept humanity in the company for over three million years, which's pretty cool.

It works.

Trust it.

Use it.

=The second principle is this: others can just love us for what we are, not what we are not. Think of that for a second.

So we can go around putting on personalities, masks, and misstatements of themselves so the world can love us. In the end, others can only love us meaningfully for what we are, not for the misrepresentation.

This is why I think that expensive cosmetic adjustments are such a misdirected use of energy and time. It's like changing the covering paper on a present-- it looks prettier for the few seconds before the gift is opened, but the contents aren't bound to change that much.

The point is this: if you like men to call you back, call them back. Treat other people the way you want to be treated. This is especially true when you are already in a relationship with a man. If you are overeager about a man and call him more than he calls you, you run the risk of killing the attraction.

Natural law holds that water flows from a higher place to a lower area. Electrical energy streams from higher voltage to lower voltage. And, similarly, the energy of attraction streams from a location of greater interest to a position of lower importance.

This means that if you want the circulation of attraction to come to you, you need to be a little less thinking about a man than he has an interest in you.

If you're into a guy and you're all over him like a hot rash before he even gets to know you, you've only tilted the tourist attraction gradient in the wrong direction. This has lots of repercussions, and none bode well for your empowerment in this relationship.

It's essential to play little of that game called hard to get' but not to the extreme. Excessive 'hard to get' will also kill the attraction. Remember the middle course—a little means returning phone calls with possibly a slight delay. Extreme is not to return it at all and expect him to call two or three times a day.

A little bit means after a reasonable date, giving him a quick kiss on the lips goodnight then running home, making him wonder. Give the man the pleasure of working for your affection.

Playing too hard to get means that you forget the benefits process. And for that reason, his efforts - the desired behavior that you want - are not getting strengthened.

This brings us to the third topic of this heading:

"Energy streams where attention goes. Except when it comes to men. When a woman puts her focus into her own life, the man's energy flows into her life; however, if she puts her attention to a man, the mangoes.

Well, I value the feedback here. Nevertheless, provided the choice of choosing universal law and your statement here, I'm will have to go with the law of gravity, the act of electricity, and energy flowing where attention goes. What I desire you to pay attention to is this: if you used a universal law and it didn't work for you, take a close look at the environment and see what failed instead of saying the code doesn't work for you.

The right man will summons the best kind of attention from the best Woman.

How to Decode What Men Mean.

When somebody says, "I'm not trying to find anything serious today," it usually means one thing: "I'm not looking for anything serious right now." Men will do just that: they will tell you what's on their mind.

Is it likely that what he means is, "Right now I'm looking for the love of my life, the person I want to settle down with completely, and you're a candidate, but I'm not going to let on lest I frighten you off?"

It's possible. But not probable.

Having been a man for over three years now, I can tell you that every time I said a woman, "I'm not trying to find anything serious right now," that's what I implied. And our friend's 29yr old buddy is stating, sure, he enjoys her business and would like more of it, but that may be the extent of what he's offering.

It's essential to take these statements from men at stated value. A propensity that I've seen among women is that they will hear this from a man, and instead of translating it at face value, they consider it as an obstacle: "Ah, but I will be the woman who will change his mind!"

So when you plan your relationship with this man to be different from what he's ready to give, you're setting yourself up for a thwarting of your expectations - and discomfort.

Another reason this is harmful is that some men (particularly knowledgeable daters) know this tendency in women and will dangle the 'severe relationship' as bait while enjoying your business without regret or fear of your departure. These situations tend to end in heartbreak for the non-male party and much self-reprisal in the form of "I don't think I did that (once again).".

Now your long-term fulfillment may be in having a dedicated relationship with a man that's heading towards marriage. And in that case, you most likely shouldn't get involved with a man who just wants to hang out with you delicately.

If you are cool with dating around and having fun, then go ahead and be cool with it. When you superimpose the expectation of something more or something else other than what's right before you, you run the risk of tainting your satisfaction, and you don't need that.

And keep in mind that dating is a skill like any other. The more you do it, the much better you get at it. So specifically, if you've run out the dating mill for a while, consider heading out on dates just for fun and learning the value of it. That way, when Mr. Right happens to supersede Mr. Right Now, you'll be better ready.

If you add a bit of 'yang' masculine energy to your interactions with men - being a bit more pro-active, happy to take some initiative, you can improve your outcomes considerably.

A bit is all it takes: just saying "hi" first, or being the first to call instead of waiting on him. It's crucial to let the total vibrant to be as the natural order of things go: you, yin; him, yang; you, the pursued; him, the pursuer. Toss in a little yang, then sit back and resume the yin position.

Self-Acceptance - How To Be Better At Dating Men Without Changing Yourself.

The world of dating can be disturbing for a single woman who is not sure of herself. All of us have insecurities, no matter how abundant, how pretty, or how smart. But there are actions you can need to make yourself comfier in yourself.

It is essential to know your strengths. You have to discover your best "you" and show the man you are dating or hoping to date this side of you. When we are comfortable, and at ease with our loved ones, many of us are at our best. How can you be comfy when you are attempting to impress somebody? Instead of trying to cover your worries, face them, and demolish them. You are more durable than them, and absolutely nothing is holding you back from meeting the man of your dreams and keeping him.

When a relationship stops working, you might ask yourself what you did wrong. It is quite natural to wish you had done some things better or differently and notice where you could improve. But it is not healthy to blame yourself or have burning regrets. You can make improvements every day and not even see it until you look back months later.

While you can approach dating in lots of ways, the traditional approach of letting a man chase you is the best way to increase desire. It might be challenging to remain a client with a man who is just unwilling to chase after you and make an effort, but that's why you have to entice him.

It's not you; it's the myths about dating that most people take for granted. It is not about ending up being someone else; it is about changing the way you date so you can reveal everyone the excellent person that you already are.

When Dating For Women, realistic Expectations

When you've been single for a long time, it's natural to question whether the reason you don't have a sweetheart right now, is that you've been too picky. Regrettably, your friend has blended opinions. How, then, can women know whether I have reasonable expectations when dating?

Do you have a perfect man in mind? A dream list of what kind of man you want and what qualities he must possess? Beware because having that kind of dream list is precisely what encourages women to have impractical expectations when dating in the first place!

Luckily, there's a third course that has led me to. To discover a relationship that brings you fantastic pleasure and fulfillment every day, you have to put your dream guy aside and consider what is ultimately the essential ingredient for a happy relationship to last;

COMPATIBILITY.

Compatibility means the two of you get along. It sounds easy, butit can be hard to discover. Still, if you want to have realistic expectations when dating, I advise you to look for compatibility first. Why? Because when all is said and done, consistency is crucial to having an enjoyable, tranquil life. With harmony, a happy marriage is a natural by-product. Without compatibility, no matter how much enjoyable you have together, no matter how fantastic the sex is, no matter how rich the two of you are, your relationship can't last.

Think about it: Constant arguing kills relationships. As good feelings fade, there is naturally less desire to spend time together.

How to know you're suitable when dating?

Ask yourself these question;

1. Do I feel unwinded around him? (e.g., can I be myself? do I find his jokes funny?).

2. Are our lifestyles comparable? (e.g., do we have the same concepts about spending and dressing?).

3. Do we have comparable tastes in food? (e.g., what sort of food do we typically eat every day?).

When dating, these criteria may look mundane as compared to other fun things. But please remember a long-lasting relationship is filled with doing day-to-day activities together. Without considering your compatibility, additional requirements have no possibility of becoming sensible expectations when dating. Choose your expectations carefully so you can have the marital relationship you've always desired.

CHAPTER FOUR

About the First Date

Dates are usually stressful. They are much more stressful for women. If you are a lady and you are opting for your first date, here are a couple of tips on how you ought to carry yourself:

Be Punctual

If your date isn't picking you up, you should never show up late. Show that you are serious and mature with the relationship by showing up early. You should call him and let him know that you are on your way if you are caught up in traffic. If your date is picking you up at your house, you need to be ready when he arrives-you shouldn't keep him waiting on you.

Be Decisive

It's common for ladies to play dumb to avoid looking bossy. If you know of the right place, you shouldn't shy away from mentioning it.

Be A Good Listener

Ladies are known to be talkative. To increase the chances of your date welcoming you for a second date, you should be a great listener. This needs you to avoid rambling on about yourself. Ask questions about the other person, if possible. As a guideline, you shouldn't butt in and tell a similar story like the one your date has just told you.

Eat As You Do At Home

Doing this makes your date think that you have food issues. To look attractive, you should eat like you usually would.

If you take alcohol, you should be cautious about it. As an important rule, you should never over-drink as you will always regret it later. It's still better to buy a diet soda than alcohol.

What Clothes To wear on a First Date - For Women!
Women are often confused about what they should wear on their first date. Below are some tips on what to wear on the first date as a woman:

Dress For The Occasion

"Fun" themed dates can take the stress out of choosing wardrobe attire. For these types of partners, wear simple fitted jeans, a flat dressy shoe, and a semi-dressy top. For more "serious dates," such as going out to dinner or a business event, dress more formally.

Avoid Being Too Sexy

Indeed, every woman wants to look attractive to their date. If you choose a revealing outfit, it may distract your date and stop him from really getting to know your personality.

Use Light Make-Up

Anything exaggerated will send the wrong signals to your date; this includes your makeup. Cosmetics ought to look appealing and natural. For the first date, avoid significant eyes by using a black pencil eyeliner instead of liquid eyeliner. Put one coat of mascara on. For the eyeshadow, ensure to choose natural shades such as light pink and brown. The crucial to making makeup look natural is to blend it entirely into the skin.

Use Light Accessories

Accessories can make up for what clothing does not have. A thin gold watch and some diamond or gem-stoned rings are enough to spice up any dress. Too much of bangles or precious jewelry can look gaudy and "low-cost."

If you are preparing yourself for your first date, you would like to know what is the best clothing to wear on a first date. Usually, it will depend on the place of the date, the time of day, and what you feel like wearing.

If you are meeting at a fine restaurant, you ought to dress appropriately. I recommend that if you are not familiar with the place, search online to find the restaurant's site and call them and see what appropriate dress code is for that place. If the area is classy, I mean using a mixed drink dress. Whether you are meeting at the bar or your date has made table reservations, a mixed drink dress is suitable for each of those two occasions.

If you are meeting at a coffeehouse, Starbucks, for example, you can use a more casual attire. High heels and a cocktail dress would look silly at a coffee store. Denim and a suitable blouse are more acceptable, although I recommend that if you want to impress your date, you need to meet him at a beautiful place where you can use an outfit that genuinely shows your womanhood.

Often people meet at odd places for a first date, such as a trekking path or a park. Make sure you dress comfortably because your date warrants a lot of walking if that's where you are going to meet your date. Denim, a comfortable t-shirt and athletic shoe, would be your best bet in this situation.

The most vital thing to keep in mind is you want to be comfortable in whatever you are using. Your clothes need to fit you just right, not too little and not too saggy.

The type of dress you will wear depends on specific reasons such as what kind of a person you are going out with or where you are going for the first date. Showing cleavage on the first date or wearing a short dress is not recommendable at all.

You can, but wear a classy casual dress or a formal dress again, depending on the person you meet. If you are going with someone senior to you like your boss, then you can wear a formal gown. If you are going with someone who is your age, then you can wear a casual dress.

Women who wear heels for the first time may walk awkwardly. Women have to practice walking until they are comfortable wearing heels.

Take a Second Date For Women
Going out on a first date is not bad, especially if you have just met online. As the date winds down, he'll let you know if he is interested in going out with you. Here are few tips for women to snatch a second date with their date.

- Going out on a very first date is hard for everyone. Now that you know this sit unwind and smile. Enjoy yourself. Even if you find him a bit strange in a charming way, you must allow him at least to show you that he's the one. Have fun. When he discovers that you are having fun, he will instantly inspire and unwind.

- Try not to make your date into a cops interrogation. You can ask questions but take a break in between. Talk about what he says, address his issues, and talk about yourself. Not too much. Just enough to go back and front to keep the conversation flowing.

Sometimes it takes longer for men to express the most basic answer to a question, so give him time and do not pressurize him to react. Get to know the man in front of you, not scare him off with your dating interrogation.

- If you enjoyed it and you want to see him once again, do not be quiet about it. Some men are timid, and they may want to say something to you, but they are not sure how you will respond. Do not worry; just throw your remark out there like "Hey, I had a great time." He will then think as to how you felt and will not leave you hanging.

For women, dating can be straightforward. Just be yourself. It is okay if you did not have an excellent time. You do not have to continue dating this person. But if you do wish to see him once again, then you must make it clear that you do. You don't want to walk away and have him think that you did not enjoy yourself when you did. Remember to leave your phone in the car because you ought to be focusing all of your attention on him. Do not take your best buddy along to analyze him before you meet. Just see what his body movement says during the night and let him know that you are interested in seeing him once again.

I've provided you some sections about spiritual principles and the metaphysics of dating. How about some straight-up technique, like things to do to make sure you have a second date after you've had an excellent first date? Here it is:

So you want a second date?

My answer: wrong question! And if you've been putting into practice what we've gone over so far, he will be the one begging to see you again. Your job is to draw him out and examine whether he's a Good Guy - and a prospective match for you.

That said, I still wish to make sure that you get the second date, so leave him wanting more (ah, that again). Remember the legend of Scheherazade in the 1001 Arabian Nights? She would tell a story to the savage King Shahryar each night and cut it off right at the cliffhanger, leaving the king in such a state of suspense that he had to approve her a day's reprieve from execution to hear the rest of the story the next day. For you, it's not your life on the line, but it is something relatively important: your satisfaction. So play your hand well and be the cliffhanger.

Whenever I give you an idea, I also like to provide concrete examples of how to use it, so here are some recommendations:

-Expose conversational loops.

What did I simply do? I opened a discussion topic - without instead completing it. That's an open loop. The unconscious mind of your listener will yearn for closure and wish to hear the rest.

" Missing info is secret, and mystery increases your attractiveness. Open some loops with the pledge of closing them later - and your King Shahryar (minus savage intent) will want to come back for more.

-Leave open physical loops. If you send great hand massages and you massage both his hands, you close the loop. If you only run one hand, he will wonder when the next hand gets the attention, and you'll have an open loop. If you kiss him goodnight on the cheek but not on the lips, you're creating an open circle. Next time, if you kiss him on the lips but keep your mouth closed, you're creating another open loop. You knew: leave him wanting more.

When you're sabotaging your fun only for the sake of kindness, you're exaggerating it. If you're dying for a hot makeout session with the man of your dreams and you know you're not going to see him until you come back from your monthlong organization journey, by all means, go all out. You can be savvy without turning into a nun.

-Hint at future shared activities. When you discover things you have in common, imagine what it would look like to do it together: "Oh my god, we need to go do a salsa class together! I love dancing and love it when a man leads well on the dance floor." Now he's imagined himself enjoying dancing with you, holding you in his arms and twirling you around, and if it does not take place, it's a viewed loss for him. People are more determined to avoid a loss than they are to go for gain, so he's now likely to want to see you again.

-Offer him an opportunity to shine. Did he say he could beat you at air hockey? That he makes a mean lasagna? Bring it on, you say - on the next date. You're giving him a possibility to show you how cool he is (men love that) and ensuring yourself a subsequent meeting, you crafty woman.

What you don't wish to do frequently is to give the man an obstacle. That's one of the emasculating habits we just covered, and it's a function of the manly - the example his man friends are for. If you challenge him, you run the risk of compromising the yin-yang polarity. You are craftily setting up an opportunity to make him look good. When he looks good, he feels great, he powers that excellent feeling to you, and he will want to see you again. And even if you're the world air-hockey champ, when you let him win (by the tiniest of margins, naturally), you both win in the long term.

Secrets to Successful Speed Dating for Women

Would you like to learn the best way to end up on someone's contact list after a speed dating event?

-Preparation, preparation, preparation

Speed dating is daunting - approximately 20 couples in a room, three to ten minutes each, and some fierce competition. How do you make yourself memorable?

Here are five tips for women;

1. Your Appearance Is Your Shop Window

Yep, that's pretty superficial, but we all know it's real, and there is no point in ignoring the fact that men will notice your looks. We are not all runway material, but knowing what your best features are, and flaunting them, means the guys won't see your flaws!

First impressions count, so make an effort with your outfit and your grooming. Ask a friend what they think about your gear before you step out of the door. Check your teeth for spinach, your nails for cleanliness, and just before you enter the venue, check your makeup.

2. Smile, be polite

Smile and the world will smile back. A happy person is mostly an attractive person, and when you've got three minutes to make an impression, your smile is the perfect starting point. And don't just smile with your mouth, laugh with your eyes. We all know when someone is faking their smile.

Be genuinely happy that you are about to meet someone new. Even if they don't turn out to be THE ONE, they might become a good friend, a new best friend, or someone you can share an interest in.

And you know, they might not be that bad! You will meet some awful men at a speed dating event. You will also meet some fabulous guys. And if you invest a little time with each speed date, you might find that beyond first impressions, a nice guy is sitting across the table.

Always appreciate them at the end of your allotted time and say it was great to meet them.

3. Spend some time in advance thinking about what you want to say about you.

Write down your life highlights (adventures, experiences, background) and some quirky, interesting facts about you. Practice speaking these things out loud - in front of a mirror!

4. Think about what you might ask your date.

Avoid questions that only need a one-word answer or block an extended response. Use words like "Tell me about ..." "What is your opinion on ..." "What would you do if ..." "Describe ... "

Also, avoid asking about jobs or previous relationships if they are a regular speed dater and don't ask.

5. Mind your body language.

Visual cues can often give away more than verbal cues. If you are disinterested or interested in them by the way your body speaks, guys can tell.

Before you go on a speed date, think about your body language and practice what you want it to say.

These are tips on how you need to act like a lady on your first date. As soon as the date is over, you shouldn't attempt to contact him if he had a good time, he will contact you. One last thing: you need not to have sex on the very first date no matter how much you like him.

CHAPTER FIVE

Essential Guide to Online Dating for Women

If you've been carefully toying with the online dating thing and have yet to find Mr. Right, then you need to relax with a cup of hot chocolate or your favorite beverage and read on. You will have a more satisfying experience once you take these tips, which we shall jointly call the essential guide to online dating for women.

Think about what you want out of the dating experience. These are the sometimes-tough questions you have to respond to before you know what you want.

Write down the features of the man you are looking for, assuming you are heterosexual, that is. Do not use generic terms. Consider things that matter most to you. You can see these "must-haves." This will let you know the kind of person you truly want, so you do not waste time on men that merely are not going to meet your requirements. Sorting with logic first will assist in eliminating untidy entanglements and give you a blueprint to follow.

Now let's get back to you. You will need a good profile to attract the type of man you want. Some times people are tempted to fudge the information in their profiles.

An excellent profile is what will separate you from other single women on your chosen dating site. Making it detailed will help bring in the best men, while, ideally, keeping away the wrong ones. Simply know that there are men who go after anything female online, just as in real life.

Write it with no slang or grammatical mistakes if you want to appear educated and severe. Listing things you like give your contacts something to discuss with you as an icebreaker. If you wish to someone financially stable with a paying task, don't be afraid to put it there!

Don't forget that men are visually oriented, and will look at your profile pictures a lot more than what you write about yourself. Using the shots taken of you in daily life is a good thing.

In general, the message here is that online dating for women can be a positive experience. Be proud of yourself, be who you are, and do not go for less than what would truly make you happy.

Online dating for women gives many chances to meet people you may not generally have an opportunity to. While some people meet at the bar or out clubbing, others do not always have time for that or aren't into that kind of thing.

This is where online dating sites can help; they give thousands of various people for your browsing discretion, all wanting to meet someone, possibly even you. The possibilities of meeting somebody are just limited by how much effort you put in.

If you're sincere and look around, you may find someone who is trying to find a lady like you, or maybe they'll find you. Whatever happens, here are a few tips to assist the process for those internet dating women out there.

- **Be Honest**

When searching for a person, you'd search for sincerity as one of his primary characteristics. Why not use the same to yourself, by using only honest info when writing your profile. Using your real age, height and weight will ensure that when a person contacts you, you know he knows what you look like.

Only use real and current pictures, as any ones from a different era of your life will simply serve in deceptive potential suitors and will only lead to awkward discussions later on when he figures out you do not look like your profile picture.

Furthermore, when putting in various other information, avoid looking like a gold-digger and asking for a man to spoil you all the time. Do not say you want to have babies or will only choose financially settled men. This will just push the agenda that you're shallow and superficial.

Rather say what you like and your aspirations in life, not what you do not want your man to do or what you can't abide (unless it's necessary).

Do not lose hope if this is a return to web dating for you. Not everything in life ends up well the first time, so keep on trying, and you'll arrive ultimately. Possibly update your pictures or profile.

- **Don't Be Afraid To Message Someone**

As soon as numerous dating websites focused on the nudge, wink, and poking of people's profiles, allowing people to others know they're were interested. It doesn't communicate much effort on behalf of the person nudging, because it's typically a one-click process.

If you truly want someone to take you seriously, try sending them a positive message, asking whether they'd like to have a discussion. There doesn't need to be any strings attached, and it's a terrific way of determining if you and he have compatible personalities before dedicating.

If you get a message from someone, avoid playing hard to get, as it is likely that the person showing interest in you will just move on. Men do not like to be messed around when looking for love.

- **Be Safe**

If you choose to meet a man in person, make sure your good friends know where you are; it's a public place and that you know well enough. As stated previously, the online is a place on privacy, and it's always much better to be safe than sorry. If you don't feel comfy or the man isn't as he described (to a severe degree), then reassess the meeting.

- **Remember Your Reasons For Internet Dating**

You are not sure of who you may find on the internet dating scene, so try to have fun and meet new people and maximize the experience.

Ever questioned why men vanish?

Do all of your relationships, "stop working to introduce"?

While many dates in other times were made within a circle of women and men who understood each other, that is not most of the case today, and checks for safe dating is necessary. Strangers satisfy in clubs and meeting areas, and many discover a date through the Internet. While you would be so unlucky to have a risk date, you must still follow all the preventative measures, and this, of course, is particularly real for women.

Here are a couple of essential tips to direct you and guarantee your security in this fast-moving modern world.

If you have a gut feeling about someone, then don't go on a date with him or her. To encourage someone to be kind to them is a bad mistake for frequently this can lead to anger and rage from the person you have wrongly dated - there are many recorded cases such as this;

- When you choose to date, then don't give away a lot of private information. Meet at a mutually agreed point instead of from your home.

- Do a pre-check on the person. Ask your friends do they understand the person how do they view him. To do this, you need to be discreet and not ask widely, but a few contacts can typically tell you enough. When dating through the net, make sure you have some genuine photos. If needed, get them to hold a paper with the date on it in a picture. There are many cases of males and females giving photographs of themselves when they were 20 years more youthful. This may sound over the net; however, you are entitled not to be fooled into meeting someone who no longer exists other than as an older man or woman. The case of one woman who reacted to an Englishman's request for a relationship - he was forty, and her photo was of forty years of age, but when she showed up in England, he discovered she was 75 years old. Difficult to believe, but it does occur.

Skype is especially important as you see the person visually while talking with them. And when you do go on that date, let one of your close buddies understand where and who you are going with and get them to call you at a proposed time for your return.

Well, all that sounds quite daunting, but the above guidance is for the worst scenario that rarely happens, but it can take place. It's up to you to safeguard yourself in the contemporary world where communities are no longer consisted of, and we reside in a world of conference strangers.

Online Golden Tips to Help Find That Special Person

Contrary to popular belief, online dating has several benefits. It's a real way by which countless women meet that unique someone. Although there are many stories about love failed online, this is more the exception than the standard. There are lots of things that women can do to increase their possibilities of forming a successful relationship with someone with whom they have met through an online dating service.

One of the most crucial things that you can do is to examine the dating site before signing up. These sites might vary considerably in terms of what the person is looking for. Getting a feel of the site and how it works before signing up can conserve a lot of time and improve the chances of finding love. Many online dating services might also offer free trials that allow you to attempt out the service before taking any type of commitment. It's a risk-free way that may lead you to the man of your dreams.

-Specify what you're searching for.

Lots of women might make the mistake of being too vague about what it is that they are looking for in a partner. Detailed information can help get rid of prospective mates that might not fit the requirements that you desire. Not only will this increase your chances of finding the best person, but it will give a positive online dating experience.

Put in the time to fill out a precise profile and attempt to address questions as soon as possible. This is a necessity when it relates to finding a partner that you will work with. Some online dating services might likewise use a personality test and matchmakings for you based on the info provided. The more comprehensive you can get, the better.

The Advantage of Online Dating For Women

Many people are getting into online dating sites to find the perfect match for them. The many online dating sites are indeed a fantastic way to connect the various people looking for a relationship.

Some women presently have been focusing on their careers more than their love life. Online dating websites have used the women greater hope and opportunities of discovering their man without changing their overall way of life they got used to.

Also, the type of process in conference men for these women depends on the screening process that they have for them. Busy women are unable to get closed with the opposite sex firstly due to the schedules and duties that they have in their hands. The online dating process is the best for them because they can know an individual more and develop the relationship romantically with a man who can be reached by e-mail or immediate messaging.

Online dating also enables the women of today to be in communication with an online partner anywhere they are as long as a computer and an Internet connection are available. It is likewise suitable for a woman to know a specific man in advance before they spend their valuable time meeting or dating.

Many online dating sites supply their members with the ability to publish an image in their profile. Many women do not feel comfy getting into a blind date, especially if they do not know how their dates may look like. Women are supplied with the knowledge or awareness of the physical features of the man that they may be interested in and are meeting soon.

Online dating also does not give a powerful dedication to the members. Women who are looking for the right man may be able to satisfy not just a single person but as many as they want.

In current days or the 1990s, all online dating was considered a new idea. Unlike today, a lot of people did not own or have access to a computer system or even have access to the web. Times have changed. Online dating is not only IN the groove; it IS the mainstream.

There are several reasons for the incredible development of online dating sites and the number of people, men and women of different ages, races, and religions who use these websites as their primary source for looking and meeting other people for that unique one. If you're a skeptic and don't believe me, just ask some of your friends in the "real" world. Many of them will tell you they have or are now using some sort of an online dating service if they are sincere.

Here are three excellent reasons why many people sign up for dating services every day:

(1) You can be confidential or not understood. You will not be asked to give your actual name, address, email address, contact number, or place of work to another online user. You, naturally, might do so but just at your own risk and choice and only when you feel safe and completely comfortable. You are not required to put an image of yourself. Publishing a photo, nevertheless, will get you more individuals thinking about your profile. So you can check out the other members on the dating website you have joined with complete privacy.

(2) You have more options online than you do in your regular everyday world. Before the world of online dating came to existence, the choice of your friends and even of irreversible partners was extremely limited to those we meet through play, school, or work. You can go through hundreds, even thousands of different people, to discover the best man only for you.

(3) The "safety problem" is the biggest reason of all, and need to be taken seriously. An online dating service will not give your details. When they get or have it, you get to choose who gets those details and.

If you are having a tough time finding the right man for you, don't misery. You can get going with online dating to find the right man for you. Many online dating services help to bring singles together. This book takes a look at some of the advantages that you can get from such dating services.

a. You can hide your identity and be anonymous. Dating sites do not need that you give your name in full in your profile. You can also exclude your full contact address. So with online dating, you can enjoy the advantage of being confidential until you choose to expose aspects of yourself to a particular date. And when you are all set to reveal more about yourself, then you actually should give the real information about yourself. Honesty is necessary here.

b. Online dating gives more choices to you than you can ever get in the real world. With online dating, you are not restricted to men within your area, work environment, or a particular social background. With online dating, you can date a man from another city and with a different way of life from yours. There are always many men, just some clicks away. And if you are one who wishes to date other men outside your country, you can say thanks to this opportunity.

Online dating also enables you as a woman to date a man at your own pace, without the pressure of any kind. This is an excellent method to "take it gradually" with dating. Stress does not help in dating, so it's a good thing that you can take your time to fall in love and show your appreciation to the man in question.

Of course, as I said briefly above, you need to be honest when engaged in online dating. You do not desire to end up being hated by your date when he finds out the fact about you. This is important when it comes to finding the right man for you.

Free Online Dating For Women is Now Much Safer

The online world has encroached into our every day resides in every aspect imaginable. The dating world ten years back was a different scene for women than it is today. Throughout those times, a lady would hook up with a person in a club, the health club, and even down their local grocery store. And while meetings of these types still go on today, what we are experiencing is more and more girls going to the Internet to find their best mate.

The advantage of these complimentary online dating for women sites is that they can search through thousands of potential mates for a guy that has similar interests to her. The issue with meeting a person through traditional methods and going out on a date with him is that if he didn't like tennis, then he might get fed up feeling like he always came second to tennis.

Of course, free online dating for women does not come without its disadvantages. The benefit of these free online dating websites for women is that you can evaluate prospective people to make sure they aren't sleazy or complete losers or are lying to you about their age etc.

Just about five years ago or so, online dating for women was filled with bad press. The media had covered a couple of circumstances of women being abducted or abused by people they met online. The issue was that free online dating sites simply didn't take the proper safety measures to secure the identity of its members. The good news is that this is becoming less of a concern. The more authoritative free online dating for women sites now makes privacy and the safety of its members their primary care. This suggests that all the personal details you get in your online dating personal profile are now protected on their encrypted servers. Only when you are ready will your email address and phone number etc. be available to the possible mate that you have been chatting with.

The current explosion of free online dating for women has enabled ladies to look beyond their local town for prospective mates. They can search for guys within a particular radius of their home town; compare with people who have comparable interests, and even between a specific age. There has never been such good potential for a lady to meet that special somebody, even their soul mate, then there is today with online dating.

Play It Safe When Dating Online

You will enjoy this post about the best online tips for women to remain safe. These tips are quite helpful when you begin dating somebody new.

It is time for you to know some of the best online tips for women to stay safe. You can use these tips to be safe when looking for that unique somebody in your life. Online dating is the most comfortable and easy service to start meeting men. It has gained appeal over the last few years. Let's discuss some security tips for online dating.

-Beware! Online daters are not always truthful: Some people attempt to discover their matches by criteria money, wealth, and position. When selecting the best ones to date, you should be careful. People tend to take advantage of using them just for specific purposes. Do not indulge in any activity without knowing the true nature of the person. Take as much time as you need to ensure that you get to see that individual along with possible. That way, you will at least have covered your basis.

-Be wise when choosing: Do not give out your personal information to any person when you are dating. Following our online dating tips for women will help keep your identity much more secure from fraudsters posing as online daters.

-Keep away from mysterious places: This is the most crucial point that has to be understood by every woman who is into online dating. Since you desire to be around familiar surroundings in case something unusual occurs, this is reliable online dating advice for women.

-Be protective: You ought to beware when you are dating online because some men are just looking for sex. You should always keep defense close at hand until you know for sure this is the right person.

Now you can know that women ought to be very cautious when they go dating. These online dating tips for women can be efficient, and you can keep this book helpful before your next online date.

With the web ending up being a part of most people's lives, online dating has developed in popularity.

Some questions that women have about online dating are:

- How do I know whether he's insane or a serial killer?

- How do I safeguard myself if my date turns hazardous?

- What do I have to do to meet the best type of people?

- How do I know if my date isn't pretending to be someone he's not?

These are just a few of the many questions that pop into women's minds whenever they think of attempting dating through the internet.

The Reality of Online Dating for Women

If you take all the essential precautions, online dating can be a fun and secure way to meet other people. It's possible to build caring and relying on online relationships that result in lasting offline relationships.

For instance, whether you're communicating in the real or virtual world, you ought to make an effort to learn more about your date. Understanding who you're dealing with is the best way to be safe while taking part in online dating.

Tips for Women Dating Online

So here are other online dating tips for women:

Don't meet your date personally immediately. Instead, take the time to know more about your new friend. Do this by communicating via e-mail. This allows you to observe any disparities about his age, look, interests, marital status, profession, etc.

- Keep personal details such as your e-mail and house addresses, contact number, your place of work, etc. private during the early stages of your relationship. Cease all interaction with anybody who pressures you to give this info or attempts to trick you into revealing it.

- Once you're comfortable talking with your online date frequently, you can move your conversations to the phone. Because you have a much better opportunity to evaluate a person's spontaneous actions against the prepared replies they give through online messaging, interacting using the phone is suitable. You can even figure out from the phone calls whether there's any chemistry between the two of you.

- Only satisfy your online date in person when you're prepared to do so. Never meet in a secluded area - no matter how comfy you are with your online date. If you're flying to another city to meet your partner, pre-arrange your transportation and hotel space.

- Dress appropriately for your first date. This is best done by not wearing any kind of clothing that reveals your lingerie or thong. If you like to dress provocative, hold off until your relationship is more recognized - if you want to pursue the relationship further.

Senior Online Dating For Women - Who To Watch Out For

There are some things that it's essential to look out for if you are a woman and you are looking to find your perfect match on a senior dating site. In general, the internet is a pretty safe place, and the things you hear about people stealing your charge card information and hacking your computer are just news.

Those kinds of things do not happen typically, and it is pretty easy to be protected from those things by using your charge card, not your debit card, and installing an excellent antivirus program on your computer.

Instead, of those concepts, what we are referring to are possible dates you may discover online. And the reality of it is that online dating websites are quite safe places. Most of these people you will meet there are just regular daily men who are using the web the same as you do to browse out a perfect match.

Here are some types of men that it is crucial to be cautious of online. And among those is the guy who never grew up.

Even if you may find it difficult to believe, there are men out there today on the senior dating sites who appear to think they are still in high school. Their just want is to conquer you with their supremacy. Think for a moment what those type of guys resembled back in school; those men who were legends in their minds.

They were the ones that believed everything was a competition. They took their ideas of winning at all costs straight from the football field or the basketball court right into their relationships. And usually, with terrible outcomes.

At first, it might have been lovely to be the object of much attention, but after a while, when everything became a competition, that sort of attitude got truly old quickly. In online dating, these guys are still out there, and here is how to find them.

The most fabulous giveaway that you will find almost immediately is that their online profiles read like a fluff-filled resume instead of a description of their life. When you see some of these profiles, you can tell immediately that it is filled with lists of things they have done in their lives, but there is nothing about how they feel or what they like.

While this sort of idea may work for getting a brand-new job, you are not on the dating site to discover a staff member; you are looking for somebody who is a perfect match for how you feel and think. And unless you enjoy competing with your dates, you would be well served to stay away from this kind of guy.

But senior dating sites can work great for finding a perfect match for you, as long as you know what to watch out for. Give them a try, and you could be seeing your perfect match soon.

CHAPTER SIX

Fly like an Eagle in the "Wingman"

The expression "I'll just wing it" has resolved the majority of the world's issues. (Say this next part in a soft, suspicious voice.).

Wait, maybe winging it is a bad idea when carrying out medical procedures or packaging parachutes or planning a war. Hmmm, Come to think of it, it's not fantastic on television, cither. Maybe the only place winging works is in the domain of relationships.

Find a wingman to help you with meeting and seducing the man of your option. Going out with a great wingman is the equivalent to packing the deck in your favor. It s cheating, and who doesn't love to cheat: you get a higher score without doing all the work. It's the equivalent of not paying retail.

Let's see who makes the best wingman.

- The wingman must remain in a relationship. If. A wingman is more effective; it assists if he's outgoing and funny.

- Your wing person should know that this is a critical mission that needs focus.

- In case there are no good boys in the hood, this wingman must be enjoyable to hang with so that the outing isn't a total waste of time.

How to Conquer your wingman.

Once the connection has been made, the wingman needs to talk you up, keep the discussion rolling through the uncomfortable phases, and then let you and your target talk. The wingman is in charge of the exchange of phone numbers or emails (if you are too shy) and, regardless of the situation, the exit plan for you both.

Why does It work?

The wingman develops a subtle blend of titillating-- I was going to rattle on here, but instead I'll say this: Two heads are much better than one, and the wingman can do the dirty work. Having a wingman takes the pressure off a first hi, and feel more at ease talking to you when you're with somebody. It is a relationship made in heaven.

Boy Mets Girl.

If a relationship were like constructing a home, dating would be laying the foundation. When a girl meets a boy and stimulates fly, it's time to prepare the foundation for a future together. The relationship could stop working, but if it does work, you wish to be ready for it. I advise going into each relationship open-minded but not blind. To do that, you need to think of how to put that cement in the smoothest way possible and make sure it dries without cracking. Now let's get started building dating.

Dating on the Clock.

Your figure is not the only hourglass; we want to turn upside down when we start dating you. I'll let you in on a secret:

Bad Boys know how many grains of sand will pass through before the end of a relationship. They've dated and flirted with so many women that they can tell precisely how long the relationship will last-- generally within the very first fifteen minutes of meeting you.

- intoxicated woman in a bar = one or two nights.

- The girl just out of college = a few months at most.

- woman between the ages of twenty-four and twenty-eight = a few weeks to a couple of months.

- separated or single mommy = a couple of months to several years, depending on her way of life.

- non-desperate, non-husband hunting woman twenty-eight-plus = open-ended.

There's some fact here because men look at relationships like business deals.

The clock starts ticking in the first few minutes. Just as you're assessing your man, he's assessing you and trying to see a possible future. But there's an essential difference: people are plotting a way to stick with you long enough to have sex, even if they do not like you or plan on having anything more than a booty call. I'm sure you knew that. They pigeonhole women into categories; every single woman is possibly "bed-able.".

The Categories;

- Keepers (attractive and enjoyable).

- Meet the moms and dads.

- Random sex partner/on-again-off- once again, relationship.

- One-to-three-month phony girlfriend.

- What was I thinking?

- Close my eyes and think of Jessica Alba.

What Men Do to Evaluate Women

I want someone severe and spontaneous. The simpler I think it would be for me to run the relationship, the sooner I will get bored, and the much shorter our relationship will be.

This might seem standard, yet women frequently never see completion coming. Do you know the number of girls who were dumped apparently for no reason? This is why. They went out of the clock. In my case, Most men wouldn't have been in nearly several drive-thru relationships if women thought about the clock and had prepared ahead.

How to Conduct an Anti-Date

Make sure you have plans right after-- you want to leave the party while you're still having a good time, so he wants more of you. It's finest to have anti-dates in the daytime or, if your schedule won't enable, as a quick drink after work.

If you want to be genuinely stringent about this, offer to share the cost. I would suggest that if he uses, let him pay; there are some things, even the anti- date should not mess with.

Once on the anti-date, forget about you and pay strict attention to him, Really listen. He'll give you heaps of info in this first hour. Glimpse in a mirror before you meet him, examine your clothing and makeup, and then drop your self-awareness. This is the time to engage him in Hghthcarted conversation that stimulates his viewpoint muscle; you want to hear his take on things. I've said this before. Listening to a man's viewpoint and getting a take on his funny bone will tell you more about him than having him recite

Choose something specific and see how he will feel about it. Let the discussion flow in whatever instructions it desires to take, but keep it fun.

Ending the Anti-Date

There are three ways you can end an anti-date, with each one depending on your gut instinct:

1. If you're uncertain, tell him you thought it was enjoyable, which he needs to call you so you can have "lunch" once again anytime soon. You're setting up a second anti-date.

2. If you hate him and want him to crawl back into the river slime from where he came alright, perhaps that's a little harsh. Let's just say you didn't strike it off. Be polite and thank him for meeting you. No need to say, "I'll talk to you soon."

3. If you like him, leave him with a sexy sign-off: a naughty smile, a couple of choice words (e.g., "I was going to fold socks before bed tonight, and now I'm distracted"), a prolonged hug, or a flash of cleavage or leg. (You know how to do that without looking obvious.)

The most significant difference between the anti-date and the one that follows is that on the next date, you have both calmly agreed that you're interested. The mood of the first real romantic encounter will then increased.

Silence Is Golden.

Silence is golden whenever:

- you are indecisive about whether to call.

- you didn't get the ambiance that he liked you that much.

- he just pissed you off, or;

- he rudely broke up with you.

Overthinking things is the root of all evil in relationships. Women like to participate in overthinking at every chance. This is mainly a killer when it comes to relationships because you'll often act as if specific fantasy scenarios were real. This can get you in problem and make you angst-ridden. It also leads to insecure phone calls and long-winded emails.

Howto Be Silent

Stop and think about what silence does to you, and know that it does the same thing to men. The best way to do that is to bite the bullet and not call up until you have let some time pass and can feel positive when you send out that email or dial that number.

Note: This doe s not include calling to vent or get closure from someone who has rudely broken up with you.

Confidence in Silence

Silence constructs self-confidence. Sometimes, we are hopeless to understand whether we're wanted, even if for no various other factors than curiosity. By permitting on your own to be silent as well as not make rash connection choices or end up being angst-ridden, you are showing that you have self-confidence in yourself and think that you are such an amazing lady that all the chips will undoubtedly drop quickly where they may. You trust yourself and also have a positive self-image.

It Ain't Easy.

The reality is, being silent when you want to call truly hard. When you're staring at the phone and thinking about how much you want to hear his voice on the other end, make yourself get up and go outside for a half-hour.

Making the Connection When He Contacts You.

When someone contacts you, it's time to make an impression that will guide the interaction in such a way that conserves time and stress.

Remember, he is not your new pen buddy. You wish to discover him and either drop him or get to date quickly.

1. Before you think about responding, ask yourself if you liked what he stated in his email.

They'll just look at your image. To weed out the La-Z-Boy recliners from the right people, ask them to go back and read your profile, and then ask what it was that they liked about you.

3. Email as if you've known him your whole life, but do not make sexual referrals. When composing and addressing e-mails, just write when you seem like it. No need to rush or play games.

If you want to organize a phone conversation within the first three emails. Newbies tend to end up stuck in prolonged e-mail discussions, so ask faster rather than later on.

5. If the call goes well, arrange for a lunch or coffee date just, making it clear that you have something to do right after. Keep it sweet and short.

When You Contact Him

Feel free to call him through email if you find a man you like.

1. Compliment him on something particular in his profile, but keep the first e-mail super short. Praise among his images, his music taste, or something funny he wrote in his profile.

2. When he composes back, ask him how online dating has been going, meaning that you are both in this together.

3, Get some fundamental security issues out of the way by asking whether he is married, whether he works, and the number of times he's been on that particular dating site.

4. Follow steps two through five in "When He Contacts You.".

Keep in mind: If you call someone when and he does not get back to you, then contact him once again.

Your Safety'Net.

Always lean towards being a bit distrusting. Here's how to deal with a security 'internet:

1. Try to get as much personal information out of him as possible, but provide extremely little of your own. Instant-messaging programs make this easier.

2. First meetings should always be in hectic public places. When you leave, don't stroll straight back to your house.

3. Get his last and first name, and browse his identity online.

4. If you can meet him only during the night, have him meet you while you're out with sweethearts.

5. Take more time to be familiar with him before you invite him back to your baby crib.

If you feel any sign that something is "not right," then cancel the date/meeting altogether. Simply say, a family emergency occurred, and you'll get back to him.

This might all sound a bit paranoid, but trust your instincts and have a safe date.

CHAPTER SEVEN

Body Beautiful; Make Up Don't Break UP

Let's start with a vital point: Never clean your make-up with soap. If you're a coal miner's daughter, you must wash with hot water and moisturize. If you've used something stubborn or water-resistant, use makeup eliminator-- or, for light makeup, an inexpensive moisturizer-- and clean it off with cotton pads. Thats it. By not scrubbing your skin with soap, you'll look young forever, assuming you don't smoke or tan too much. Well, your beauty regimen has a lot to do with your long- and short-term success in relationships.

Makeup and Women

When women generally spend a long time on their makeup regimens, men also don't like it. We get irritated that you're hogging the bathroom and impatient when we want to leave now, and you need forty more minutes. Too much primp time is also dangerous because spending enough time on something so shallow can give your man the impression that your concerns are warped.

The Trick to an Easy Routine

When you're seeing a new guy, go to the first few dates in subtle makeup. He should see the real you early on, with as little makeup as possible. Let him succumb to the sexiest natural variation of you. If you doll yourself up the first four times he sees you (clown makeup), you'll need to keep that up for the rest of the relationship. Your natural look is simple for you to maintain, and the bonus offer is that when you have all glammed up for a party or wedding event, he'll think you're a new woman.

The lesson to the story is that you should look the way you want to be dealt with. Going natural is not the single ticket to the train, but if you are naturally well-groomed, men will pick up on that and respond by treating you like you look:

-How Fitness Affects Your Love Life

There is no best way of saying this: the much better you view, the higher the variety of men who will find you appealing. The same holds for men, but as you probably now know, men are a little more shallow and less flexible when it comes to looks. As I repeat over and over again, men are visual animals! So you need to look good, And still, the more men you draw in, the more choices you'll have. By being in shape, you'll give yourself the best opportunity of meeting that special somebody you have chemistry with, of entering into that fantastic relationship that doesn't make you "settle." You do not want to be the "last lady chose." And the way to avoid that is to keep fit.

The good news is that any in-shape, the well-groomed body can be appealing to hordes of men. Yes, it takes work and, it takes commitment, but the rewards far surpass the effort. Stop making a statement like, "I want someone to like me for who I am within.".

You need to note that being liked for who you are within is very important, but you could be the best vehicle on the lot, and if you're not a little shiny on the outside, a prospective buyer will never assess under your hood and take you for a spin.

You Are What You Think

When you stroll into space, focus your mind on something attractive, confident, and naughty. This is yet another reason to do the right lingerie and get a fresh pedicure, even if no one will see them feeling confident is much simpler if you're dressed for success.

Things to consider consist of:

- stuff you find romantic (dinner for 2, strolls on the beach, anything);.

- a fantasy about the guy across the room-- let your mind drift; or.

- cut to the chase and simply think about sex.

Strangers have no concept of what your strengths or weaknesses are, so if you're thinking sexy and robust ideas, you will be viewed as intense and hot. Other women won't have the ability to pick up on your mindset, but the young boys will.

Body Stance.

Have you ever observed how you walk when you're happy against when you're unhappy? Have you ever imagined other peoples feelings by the way they're standing? You know you have. Check out these three secrets to attractive body movement:

1. Great posture: Stand straight and relax your shoulders and facial muscles.

2. Slow walk: Move a touch slower than usual.

3. Body awareness: Ensure you feel what your body's doing as it moves. Focus on your hip flexors and neck.

Confidence Is Sexy!

What Not to Do

These are all significant turnoffs, antithetical to sexiness:

- slouching;
- shifty eyes and lack of eye contact;
- an uptight stance or stiff gait.
- stressed-out behavior; an upset, irritated, or troubled facial expression; and,
- any wallflower habits, such as leaning against a wall or avoiding the crowd.

The Eyes Have It.

Simply hold a mild think and look of something naughty, even if your conquest is telling you about his toolbox. He might also ask you what you are thinking-- but he most likely will not, for worry that he's wrong. If he asks, your response always needs to be, "Oh, I'm just listening to you and thinking about what you're saying.".

Perception is often higher than reality, and now it's time to use it to your advantage.

Second Base.

Remember first, second, and third base? I'm not talking about baseball I'm speaking about how far you let a man choose you.

The first step is kissing, the second step is touching over the clothing, the third step is touching under the clothes, and a home run is, well, a crowning achievement!

When things were simpler, it's easier to go back in time. Take high school, for instance, where a day's education consisted of cheating on a mathematics test, putting a live rat in the teacher's cars, and making out with a hot alternative

Relationship Time Machine.

It's easier than you think to return to the days when you had an unwritten schedule of how long it should take to go from base to base. There's no need to pitch the idea of going back to "high school." Simply walk him to the first step, with a prospective perk of making in the backseat of a car. The n "swing" a little harder on each date, consequently letting him know there's more on deck if he's a star player-.

When you keep the ball with your group, Baseball works in your favor. Move from base to base at every speed you are comfy with, letting him take a base occasionally to get more caring with each date. You can get to know him much better and decide whether to go for the grand slam with bases filled or to cut it short and tag him out at second instance. Either way, you'll always depend on the bat.

The Sexual Dance in Three Steps.

Step 1: Teasing.

Similar to you need to "get into the state of mind," men need to be lured well before bedtime. This is especially real in long-lasting relationships. Do this by carrying out the cliched act of teasing. Examples include:

- Walking to the refrigerator naked.

- Bending right from the waist instead of the knees.

- Dressing in such a way that is abnormally sexually intriguing for your wardrobe.

- Slapping his ass romantically or doing something physical that a man would generally do to a woman.

Step 2: Resisting.

Withstand him if he attempts to return your gestures, but do it in a teasing way.

- If he attempts to kiss or caress you, feel free to kiss him back and start moving a way that is hot and bothered; then smile and leave.

- If he is aggressive about the process, fight him off in a playful way, but withstand arrest; this helps to increase his desire to keep pursuing you.

Step 3: Giving In

When you finally give up, it ought to make him feel as if he's conquered you even if it's just for the very first few minutes of the session.

Let him think or believe he's getting away with something. Once things are underway, feel free to jump his bones.

The three-step process is not implied to be demeaning to women. It merely uses a man's natural desire to pursue sex by giving him the chance to do it. There are other significant ways to keep the sex exciting, such as a series of touch-and-go quickies, which can also keep that muscle in good condition. But the three-step process is an attempted- and-true one that you can use for any relationship at any stage. If a man doesn't wish to make love with you, attempt these three actions, and if he still reluctant or doesn't want to, drop him or get it somewhere else. That's what men do.

Find ways to make him pursue you a little bit more than you are pursuing him-- this will successfully keep him on the prowl.

CHAPTER EIGHT

Text Messaging

Text messaging, or as I like to refer to it, "sext messaging," is not just a fad. It's the most prominent form of foreplay considering that kissing.

In this chapter, we're going to consider text messaging as a tool in seduction and dating. You will also learn when to send naughty photos.

Foreplay

Words are valid, and if you choose the right ones at the right time, they can have a tantalizing effect. Keep your messages sweet and brief, pick phrases that are more suggestive than apparent, and always keep in mind that he might not be the only one who reads them that need to conserve you some carpal tunnel problems.

- "I woke up thinking about you ... mmmm.".

- "I have something I wish to show you;--".

- "It's kind of hard to text with just one hand ... hee nee.".

- One loves the way you feel.".

- "Thank you.".

Those naughty short messages received while your man's at work or out with friends can get his wheels spinning in your direction. Receiving text messages is also incredibly intimate because the whole exchange happens internally: he's not reading it aloud, so you're literally getting in his head! Consider that the next time your thumbs are dancing on the keypad.

Sexting Images.

Seducing with sext messages is a skill that needs understanding your man and specifying the personal borders you like. I've currently explained that using the right words can be a potent stimulator, add the best photo, and you're lethal. But if you choose to send pictures, attempt to get him to send a compromising photo of himself first. Never hurts to have collateral!

- Send photos just after you trust him.

- Pictures are better delivered with comic captions; sex and humour are a man's favorite activity.

- Never add your face or any identifying information, such as tattoos, identifiable places or objects in the background, or fashion jewelry.

- In general, women dating more youthful men (sixteen to thirty- 2) must not send out images that they wouldn't want the whole world to see. Simply put, make sure your guy is matureenough not to reveal all his friends, but expect that he's going to show at least one friend.

- Explain the fact that any exploitation of your personaltext messages is a deal-breaker, which he'll be walking if he breaks this code of trust.

Baiting.

Text messaging can also be used to bait somebody. This takes a certain quantity of creativity and storytelling skill. I call this the "I understand something you don't know" approach. It's sophomoric, but it works. Here's how you do it:

1. Think of a sexy story and fantasy.

2. Administer the story in little parts through text. Start by sending out a text that states something like, "I've got to inform you something." Simply leave it at that, and he'll react with "What?".

3. You react with, "I'll text you in a minute." The point is to get him intrigued in something you have to say, to bait him into playing along gradually.

4. Chances are he will call you and ask you to sayit verbally. This you need to resist. Do nottalkon the phone.

5. As soon as you have him hooked, text the fantasy in little, three- to ten-word bits. He'll respond like among Pavlov's pet dogs.

The more imaginative you become, the more fun you will have. You will also have a chance to exercise the power of leading him around. It's a great deal.

Why Men Use Text Messaging.

The majority of men use texting as a weapon in their dating toolbox. Here's why:

- they can text from almost anywhere, such as while they're on a date and the lady is in the ladies' room, while they're at work, or while they're sitting on the sofa enjoying the game.

- It's sly, and people love sly.

- It does not need talking on the phone.

- It makes it simpler to lie.

- There is no form of background noise or anything else that would indicate where they are.

-They can quickly communicate with approximately tendifferent women.

(maybe more, if we type fast!).

- Booty texting prevents the risk of rejection over the phone.

- We love having a picture of you naked on our phones. This works primarily in your favor. Insight, in mind.

Texting Isn't a Replacement for Talking.

Are you worried that your man only texts you? Make sure you have him trained to call and communicate in an individual right from the beginning of the relationship. Compliment him when he calls, and do not text back when he hasn't called.

In other words, train him to call you. Making the right call on calling and texting usually depends on the situation. I'm giving you standards to draw on when you're not sure, but in general, trust your instincts. Things can get out of hand the other way if you do not have a rule of thumb in place. Texting ought to be used to boost seduction, not as a surrogate kind of human interaction!

These days, we are interacting regularly but stating less. Quick communication isn't alwaysexcellent communication. As long as people have blood in their veins and air in their lungs, there will be no replacement for human contact.

Difficult Call

Nature weeds out the weak birds, plants, and pests by permitting only the strong-- and smart-- to survive. Males and female do the same thing to each other, with each forcing the other to survive through a series of relationship tests. Similar to the squirrel that misjudges a branch-to-branch leap is a goner, the guy who neglects your emotional signals is also a goner.

Although these tests do not have life-and-death consequences, they're still essential. In most relationships, the woman tests the man to see if he's alpha enough oreven conscious of her needs.

Edgy men and bad young boys will often turn the tables and decide to test you. You may find this annoying, so I'll describe why and how men do it so you can understand how to respond.

Why do men do this?

- Men end up being so experienced at winning women they're trying to look for a difficulty;

- Men are much more likely to show their true colors when pissed off; and.

- Men want a fast way to see where your weak points and strengths lie.

Have you ever been with a man who, all of a sudden,looks intentionally adversarial in a conversation, pressing your buttons (albeit never physically)? (You'll know he's not checking you.

CHAPTER NINE

Dating Rules Women Must Follow

If you are set to go on your first date, you may be anxious. You are wondering what to talk about, what to wear, or will he kiss you.Youwould like to make a good impression and ideally make it to a second date.

That is all fine and well, but it leads me to rule #1.

Forget about impressing him. You are the selector here.

The best way to approach date number one is to be yourself and don't worry about impressing him. Men like it when you notice little things they do. This is one of the big first date guidelines for women.

Don't talk about your ex. Nothing, nada, zip, zilch, not one word. This is a substantial turn off. People often like to talk about themselves and they truly don't wish to find out about your ex and how he did you incorrect. It reveals you in a very extremely unappealing light.

Don't inform him what sort of man you are looking for. Redirect it if at all possible if the conversation heads in this direction. Let him wonder what type of man you are seeking and let him question if it could be him. You don't need to inform him you are trying to find a man who is faithful, sincere, effort yada yada. This all goes without saying. Don't provide him any ideas, you wish to see what sort of man he is, not a man who will attempt to be what you desire him to be.

Do not interrupt and talk about yourself when he is talking about him. If he simply shared a story and you have one similar, keep it to yourself up until he is finished talking.

Men run from feeling. You have a lot of time to tell him later after you have him hooked about how your daddy abandoned you or whatever. Dates aren't a place for him.

A smile has the tendency to say more than words ever could. It shows you in a warm, attractive light.

Do not bring up the future. This very first date rule for women is enormous and is the number one place they mess up. You do not ask him when is he going to call. You don't ask him when will you see him again, and you do not ask him crap about the future where you and he are concerned. This tells him he has the power to dictate the regards to how this goes. He doesn't, you do.

The secret to a very successful first date is in your attitude. Most times, women wonder and sit if the guy will ever call them again, and they start to analyze every minute of the date.

Instead of wondering if he will call again, picture him questioning if you will accept a second date. Seriously, women invest much time obsessing over men. The best first date rule for women would be in your mind.

Dating Rules For Women To Follow

Maybe you have interacted with, or perhaps have friends who just merely appear programmed to be at ease with themselves, but are drop-dead stunning with minimal effort? Has it blown your mind to contemplate utterly how effortless it truly is for some women to be themselves whileattractingguys left and right?

Are they merely endowed with ridiculous fortune, or are they onto a little something you're not?

Let's concentrate on some essential dating guidelines for women that establish surefire destination with the opposing sex:

Consider Yourself as a Treasure, and He'll Follow Suit

An attractive female knows that she's deserving enough of a man's time, commitment, and, most significantly, his RESPECT. Because she feels as though a romantic relationship might conserve her, she never aims for a gentleman simply because she feels as though a romantic relationship could save her.

The fact is, her everyday life is so fulfilled that she doesn't demand a man to repair her or even make her complete. A sassy gal is completely alright remaining single at the moment, mainlybecause she is aware that Mr. Right will come in due course.

Generally, there isn't any need to bein panic mode or even reduce your expectations to create room for a man who won't take care of you in the way you should be taken care of. Most importantly, you don't consider attracting a guy out of desperation, for the easy reason that isn't a particularly appealing quality.

It's vital to be a self-referenced female who doesn't look for out a person through public opinions. She will allow a gentleman into her life even if he tends to make her happy and also boosts her individual growth.

Her romantic relationship does not specify her existence but also improves it. The difficulty with numerous women is the fact that they frequently date a man for the previous reason rather than the latter.

They'll behave desperatelyand clingy just because they're deathly scared of being alone, even though this indicates lessening their expectations together with putting up with just any guy that comes their way.

Behaving out of fear can never be the foundation for a healthy, long-lasting romantic relationship!

To put it simply, self-esteem is accomplished by placing worth on yourself, which subsequently will cause a quality guy to address you in the sameway. Otherwise, an appealing lady does not have any issues showing him the front door and hence moving forward with her own life.

Just Say "NO" to The Head Games

The folly of manipulating a man is the fact that every happiness and joy you'll get out of toying with his head will likely be SHORT-LIVEDAfter you've dealt him your best cards and he's abandoned chasing you;consequently there won't be much desire to stick around.

For that reason, do not bother abiding by a handful of absurd guidelines. There's an abundance of destructive recommendations swimming out there, which are usually established out of specific experiences that don't deal with everyone. You may hear that you should not kiss on a very first date, or even that you have to go to bed with him on the third date.

Please, all these so-called standards are produced by bitter and jaded people who wish to secure themselves from getting scorched again. Following all these will just lead to game-playing, which is just another term for "manipulation".

As I've said, deception does not have any place in a healthy romantic relationship, and anything based upon a lie will inevitably rip apart in the future. That's precisely why it's more important to be a well-balancedgirl instead. Which means no playing "hard to get," nor should you offer him with virtually no difficulty at all.

An attractive woman is who she is partial because she knows how to strike the middle ground: she does not muddle with a man's head; neither is she effortlessly won over.

Get Your Mind Out of the Clouds

You are mindful, great deals of relationship problems come from bearing impractical expectations. You're keeping quality guys out of your life anytime you get trapped by fantasizing about unattainable stereotypes.

That's mainly because none of them can compare well to the suitable (extremely best) man residence inside that dream world of yours! Truthfully, you should learn how to temper your expectations with an awareness of usefulness.

In a parallel galaxy, all the men you'll meet have big arms, 6-pack abs, spectacular ripped appearances, and limitless wealth. You might think that meeting each of those attributes is the solution to an excellent relationship, but it's much more than that.

Ask this question: "Am I going to have a happy romantic relationship if my man didn't have (insert quality here)?" You can either make your expectations more reasonable or simply cross out that specific characteristic entirely if this is so. If not, then guarantee that it is on your list and then continue to your many other expectations.

Go down your list and implement the basics. In something like 20 years from now, will the perfect image body still be considerable, contrary to psychological maturity, reliability, or perhaps stability? Consider that for a while!

You're not living in a motion picture here - it is the real-world you're in. Don't procrastinate for a brave knight to arrive barging in and saving you from the drudge of your everyday life.

You'll have to do that for yourself!

Derive Pleasure As Well As Satisfaction From Your Daily Life, Not A Romantic Relationship

While a sassy gal will always create space for a worthwhile man in her life, she's not ready to flip her routine upside-down just to meet his personal preferences. She has the guts to continue living the way she was before they met.

It's exceptionally crucial not to lose focus on the extra elements of your life when you are getting into a romantic relationship. As we've said, your life ought to focus on what is most effective for you.

Make sure you have your top priorities sorted and also don't get the practice of dropping everything else just for him. However, it's okay sometimes to leave valuable time for yourself and enough room for customized growth.

That's the concern with lots of females - as soon as a guy enters the photo, practically everything goes haywire. They fail to remember their family and friends, slack off at the workplace and even permanently drop off the face of the Planet.

That's not therightsolution to live your everyday life. A romantic relationship ought to highlight the quality of your life and hence inspire you to perform better.

Going back to what I mentioned in the past, whether or not you have got a boyfriend presently shouldn't influence the big photo.

The best dating rule for women is to stabilize your top priorities by continuing to keep him in the loop but not to the point in which he's now disrupting your daily life.

Returning to our middle-ground metaphor, discover ways to go out of your way when suitable buy at the same time, stay away from appearing too scarce. Don't hide from him simply to observe precisely how far he'll chase after you. You're better off buying a dog if you're into that type of thing.

Comparable to men, there are rules the ladies can play in a relationship. These are thought-about standards in society and are valuable in figuring out whether their relationships can continue. Dating can be likened to a game, and in any game, there are winners and losers. These guidelines can make the lady a winner.

The girl should always look good. Use beautiful clothes, make sure the hair is in good shape, and use lipsticks. Everywhere in the world, there are men approaching women straight for a possibility to start a relationship.

Do not expose excessive details about yourself. This includes giving your house phone number and your email address. Men always like mysterious women.

If you are a woman that is slim no matter how you eat, that's great, But the big ones need to work on their bodies to be in shape. And men do mind the bodies of their dates.

Let him use to spend on your meals and everything, by doing this, no matter what the outcome of the relationship, you will not lose.

Show that you like flowers. And let him buy some for you.

Do not turn up early for dates. Keep him waiting. You are the one being chased after.

Never be exceeding available. A girl with no life does not sound exciting.

Do not let the dates be a drag. Short and interesting will keep them wanting more. If it feels like the meeting is too long, suggest you are not feeling well in a ladylike manner.

Men are proud beings, so never talk about your ex-boyfriends. He does not need to know that other guys had spent time with you, and he will not like to know either.

Never offer or give in to a request to sex too soon. That can lead to a premature "game over."

Be courteous. Never criticize his friends and family. That will not make him change anyway, so avoid getting a frown from your man.

When it comes to online dating, there are some standards too. Never give away your primary email until you have chosen the man to be your boyfriend or a friend. In online mode, it is still the lady who must be chased.

He's picking you up for another date. Maybe it's the second date, or perhaps it the fourth or fifth one. The dating rules for women can be so complicated in some cases, and the path to his heart is littered with them.

Dress Your Best - Looks Matters

Looks aren't everything, so they say, but the fact is that excellent health, neat look, and an enjoyable body smell work in your favor. Take a while to make yourself look attractive and stylish. Your date will appreciate the effort. Men often love a woman who genuinely cares about her appearance and wellness and will be incredibly drawn into you.

Confidence Make A Woman Glow

Confidence is needed from you to win at making him yours. Self-confidence is hot.

Men are brought into a positive woman, so if this is a weak area for you, then find out how to acquire self-confidence. Self-confidence is just being sure of who you are, what your strengths are, and how important you are.

-Give Him a Stimulating Conversation

In addition to being attractive and lovely, you should have the ability to hold an intriguing, engaging conversation with men. If you can make a man laugh, talk, and enjoy himself as much as he does for you, then you're getting significant headway in the game of love. The more you're able to do this, then the more you're ready to pull him into another date, repeatedly, always.

Discuss some amusing times you've had, and perhaps even a couple of embarrassing ones, but do not get too personal. Keep backward and forward going, and handle the ball well when it's in your court before passing it back to him.

-Smile Often - You're Beautiful

Men love a woman who loves to smile. It can brighten up his day and yours - and smiles always put the smiler in agood mood immediately. Reveal those sexy pearly whites.

As you can see, revealing your best shots to win a man isn't difficult. The Dating rules for women can bedifferent, but learning to smile, radiate confidence, and be a fantastic conversationalist can go a long way.

How many times we watch these scenes in the films, the first date alwayscreates lots of butterflies in the stomach, regardless of the gender of the person. If you are a woman who wants to date thoroughly, then you can discover the many rules that would guide you through the beautiful game of dating.

- **Safety first:**

If it is your first date or you are frequently dating consistently with aman, then be sure of your safety initially. Never reveal all your personal information on the first date itself. He will be patient to check out more about the personal side of the man you have chosen real.

- Find common ground: Being a lady, you should feel comfortable about the place and atmosphere of the date. Do not go for candle-light dinner or long drives on dates. Identify what you both would enjoy and meet at sites of common interest, such as art museums, parks, and so on. This could also be a joint sports event such as playing tennis, table tennis, or just shooting darts.

- **Enjoy yourself:**

Make sure you have fun when being with your man. Men like to be in the company of attracting, well-groomed ladies.

- **Involve in activities**: If you are anxious being with a man and talking with a man, ensure you invite him to one of your favorite activities, such as walk in the park, horse riding, etc.

You may be doing it the wrongway, or you may justneed some dating rules that will make the process a little easier. Follow theserules and see your dating life change much faster than you expected.

- **Know what you desire.**

It sounds too simple, but you have to know what you want and stick to it. If you are just looking for something casual, stick to it, and do not let relationship-type guys into your life, or you will be the cause of heartache. If you are looking for a long-lasting man, leaping into bed with the first individual that asks you out sends out the message that you desire a fling. Know what you want, and stick to it.

- **Love yourself**

This seems to be the one of dating advice for women that women want to skip. We are in an age of pleasure principle, and many people are trying to find something fast and easy. Love yourself. It will subconsciously send out the message to men that you are a positive woman who deserves dating.

- Know how to look fantastic.

Get it if you need assistance with people design or grooming. There's absolutely nothing bad with calling on the professionals to do so. You may buy a new wardrobe if you are new to the scene, or just get some advice on how to combine what you already have. Establish an appearance that makes you feel fantastic.

Start using underwear more frequently not because you are going to delve into bed with each man you come in contact with unless that's the dating life you want, butbecause it does something to your self-esteem that makes you more noticeable when you walk into a room. It's a little style tip that includes self-confidence in a heartbeat. Even when you have pretty lacy things beneath your Juicy Couture tracksuit, you immediately feel sexier. And when you feel hot, you act attractive, and men love that.

- **Don't sweat the little stuff.**

When it comes to design, style, and beauty, obsessing over the reality that your eyebrows didn't get waxed uniformly is going to take your focus far from a really terrific date. At the same time, if you are flipping out all night because the waiter spilled water on the table, you aren't going to see your date's remarkable discussion. Don't sweat the small things.

If you are looking for a short-term person who does not take dating seriously, put yourself where they are 3/4 the bars, the clubs, and dance joints. The point is to effectively date, you need to meet men, and that isn't going to happen while you are at home surfing the Internet.

The Bottom Line

The dating process in the 21st century is quite easiersaid than done, not just for women, but for men too. The best dating tips for women in the 21st century include tips that help women in being a 21st-century woman, without looking too eager. She needs to know precisely what she wants while having the self-confidence to pursue it. Ensure you look great, always love yourself, and put yourself out there, and it will not be long before you meet a man who will want to have dinner with you. And a little lingerie has not injured any person.

CHAPTER TEN

Dating Game

Life is full of games. From the Xbox to rock-paper-scissors, humans play games all the time. What makes you think that games would drop in matters of the heart? They don't.

Even though we all say that we dislike playing games, all of us do it. What we hate are uninteresting games > bad Players, or, worse, losing. The most challenging thing about the dating game is that the guidelines are foggy at best and, reality be told, the question of who wins is somehow subjective. However, we all know what it looks like to lose. So, we need not do that anymore, I'm going to show you how to give yourself the best chance at winning.

Games in Nature.

To understand how to be an efficient player in the dating game, you need to know nature. In the animal kingdom, various types have created some incredibly creative ways of courting: a doe will speed for weeks to tease a dollar, salmon will swim countless miles to pass away and generate, and penguins will stand in the cold for months.

We are notdifferent. Our mating rites are just as wacky. And just as predictable. Human beings happen to produce several predictable-- and even instilled-- reactions to all sorts of stimuli.

The Game Plan: Playing to Win.

Here's your plan of five strategies for coming and winning out on top-- pun intended. The trick is to blend in many game techniques that he becomes stunned, and then becomes your puppy - family pet. If he's wise and tough, he'll be a deserving opponent, and you two will have a blast. The critical thing to keep in mind is to have a good time and consider it as just a game when you are in the middle of it. That won't always be easy. The good news is that sometimes nature tosses us a bone of simplicity. Occasionally everything is perfect, and you do not need too many checks and balances. In the meantime, but you have to keep your self-confidence undamaged and your video game face on, so listen up. Your strategies are:

- unpredictability and spontaneity;

- developing guidelines for the sole function of breaking them;

- not calling;

- using sexy words; and.

- releasing sex as a weapon-- in some cases.

Unpredictability and Spontaneity.

One thing is for sure: humans aremostly curious. Take advantage of that by keeping your man off guard, off-balance, and always wondering. The bestway this can be done effectively is as follows:

1. Always dress attractive, but never in the same style..

2. Never call, e-mail, or text him in any predictable way.This means that you must call whenever you want to call (within reason) or not at all. Say, for example, you would generally call just after work if you got a message from him,instead, call him during the day or early the next morning.

Handle it around a bit; never let him have the ability to "anticipate" your call. He calls you text. He e-mails, you call. He texts, you e-mail two days later You may even choose not to call at all. This inconsistency is lethal in agood way

3. Be on time for dates and cancel sometimes. Being on time is not usual when it comes to women (sorry, but it's true), so this will set you apart and get him believing. As soon as in a while, and cancel. The rightway to cancel for the most impact is by setting up something for a night when you have plans to do something else (he does not know this), and after that, cancel and say sorry. Remember that you don't want to be impolite by cancelling at the last minute: Cancel the night before or very

early in the morning. Do this by phone; do not text or email! Calling shows that you have balls.

4. Blurt out some sort of obscenity or outrageous comment if you're not naughty by nature. Do not overdo it * Just make it visibly racier than usual.

5. Ask him out. Ask him on a date. Simply shrug it off and do not return his calls for a few days if he says no. You wish to get this tiger to jump through hoops for you, so you need to be proactive here.

Above all, you do not want your man/victim to notice any patterns about you, because if he does, he'll quickly settle on those patterns-- and after that lose interest. In other words, you wish to keep him from figuring you out for as long as possible. It s constant spontaneity, as I've saidearlier.

Making Rules for Breaking

Hypocrisy gets men upset just as women; double standards are a hot point for everybody. If you practice hypocrisy in the right way,it will get your man on the warpath, where he is actively looking to understand how you can get away with something. You provoke this by creating guidelines that you know are okay for women to break, but not for men.

- Make a rule that the man can't use his phone at the table while you're eating. When your phone rings, answer it but keep the discussion super quick. If he questions the hypocrisy, just respond like, "Girls talk on the phone more than men. We can't help it, sorry. I will not do it again.".

- Say that you do not truly like kissing in public, and after that plant one on him. Tell him you couldn't help yourself.

- Have him assist you in lifting something in your house because you can't lift it. Then raise how intense you foci from going to the gum.

Employing hypocrisy as one of your subtler strategics can toss off his game strategy. This is "hypocritical hardball," and it may be the thing that keeps you from being eradicated to left field.

Keep in mind that these "guidelines for breaking" are adorable and fun, and much different from the limits and standards you put down for your relationship. Make sure he can discriminate. Also, you want to use the "good for ladies, not good for people" thing moderately, as you don't want him to get so upset that he drops you.

Not Calling.

I start this area with a warning: Keep in mind that he might "not call" you, too. Calling is a two-way street, and you do not wish to let this strategy backfire. If you see he was not calling when he said he would or is following the three-day rule or another approach, then beat him at his own game by referring back to the ideas under "Unpredictability." (Guys love to hate this.) Or try these strategies:

1. Don't require a day after he's left a message.

2. If he sends you text-messagesand asks you to call, don't call him. And do not text him back, either.

3. If he gives you a call and you're somehow "busy" or on the phone, call him back at a random time and day.

4. Describe number 2 under "Unpredictability and Spontaneity." Similar to everything I'm teaching you, use "not calling" sparingly-- its enough to effectively keep him on his toes.

Using Sexy Words.

The words you make use of are as important as what you discuss. One good strategy to keep relations calm is to direct your intensity at the topic of conversation topic, not at him. However, the most powerful way to use words is sexual. There are a few words that, when falling from a woman's lips, drive men crazy.

- Panties.

- Thong.

- Sex.

- Tits.

- Ass.

- (Any word used to describe sex or a woman's body or underwear will be enough here).

By sprinkling your discussion with these words, you make his mind drift onto sexual subjects. You are managing his ideas, which gives you the edge.

Deploying Sex as a Weapon.

Consider yourself warned: This is the way you do it without painting yourself into a sexual corner, appearing to be a tease, or becoming the object of a grudge:

- Be sexually flirtatious, but not too flirty. Thumbs-down includes flashing him, overtly touching him, or guaranteeing anything specific.

- If you are all ready to make love, then do fast your terms.

- If he gets you upset or hasn't been attentive, tell him that you need to be in the state of mind, which because of his inappropriate actions, you are not in the state of mind. No need to take one for the group here. Reschedule your session.

- Be intimate at unexpectedtimes and in unforeseen locations.

Question &Answer.

Q:1 doesn't like playing games. Why should I follow this guidance, considering that it appears like a lot of game-playing?

A: Games are enjoyable. If it does not feel enjoyable, then possibilities are you're not playing correctly, or you're playing with somebody who cheats. You should find someone with whom you love playing the game-- and then have fun and relax.

The trick to playing-- and winning-- the game is paying attention and understanding human nature. Offer as little info about yourself as possible while, in turn, learning more about him than his mom. It s a game, and the overtone must always be a wink and a laugh, signaling that you are just having fun.

Just like any game, practice makes perfect. There will be moments of angst, intrigue, and second-guessing, but when you get much better, you'll begin to see it for what it is: exhilarating!

www.ingramcontent.com/pod-product-compliance
Lightning Source LLC
LaVergne TN
LVHW011719060526
838200LV00051B/2957